LITERATURE-BASED
SCIENCE

LITERATURE-BASED SCIENCE

Children's Books and Activities to Enrich the K-5 Curriculum

by
Christine Roots Hefner
and
Kathryn Roots Lewis

Oryx Press
1995

The rare Arabian Oryx is believed to have inspired the myth of the unicorn. This desert antelope became virtually extinct in the early 1960s. At that time several groups of international conservationists arranged to have 9 animals sent to the Phoenix Zoo to be the nucleus of a captive breeding herd. Today the Oryx population is nearly 1000 and over 500 have been returned to reserves in the Middle East.

© 1995 by The Oryx Press
4041 North Central at Indian School Road
Phoenix, Arizona 85012-3397

Published simultaneously in Canada
Printed and Bound in the United States of America

∞ The paper used in this publication meets the minimum requirements of American National Standard for Information Science—Permanence of Paper for Printed Library Materials, ANSI Z39.48, 1984.

Library of Congress Cataloging-in-Publication Data
Hefner, Christine Roots.
    Literature-based science : children's books and activities to enrich the K-5 curriculum / Christine Roots Hefner and Kathryn Roots Lewis.
        p.   cm.
    Includes index.
    ISBN 0-89774-741-0
    1. Science—Study and teaching (Elementary). 2. Science—Juvenile literature—Bibliography. 3. Children—Books and reading. 4. Children's literature—Study and teaching (Elementary). 5. Education, Elementary—Activity programs. I. Lewis, Kathryn Roots. II. Title.
LB1585.H44   1995
372.3'5044—dc20   94-44843
                                                                                        CIP

Dedicated to our families:
Bill and Jean
Charles and Steven
Jeff, Michael, and Elizabeth

Special thanks to our mentors:
Dr. Judi Ford
the late Dr. Mildred Laughlin
and
Anne Masters

CONTENTS

INTRODUCTION

Why Use Children's Literature to Teach Science?

Science is everywhere. Science influences our every breath. Science is an integral part of our existence. As Deborah C. Fort so aptly puts it, "The science to which all should be exposed in all environments is uncompartmentalized; it is everywhere."[1]

Science is the key to solving the world's most critical dilemmas and challenges: overpopulation, hunger, pollution, disease, endangered species, and uncharted territory. Perhaps the best way to ensure a healthy future is to equip our children to become scientific problem solvers by giving them the higher-order thinking skills and a working knowledge of the scientific method. As Fort says, "If the large majority of tomorrow's citizens don't achieve scientific literacy, society may be in peril, for ignorance in the postindustrial era can devastate the planet."[2] Education's challenge is to teach students how to look to science for solutions to problems. The science challenge is a growing national concern addressed by Goal 4 in the Department of Education's *America 2000: An Educational Strategy:* "By the year 2000, U.S. students will be first in the world in science and mathematics achievement."[3]

Literature-Based Science encourages teachers to intertwine literature and science. The partnership of these two disciplines seems natural. Fort writes, "One way to approach it [science] is through the broadest possible curriculum in the elementary and early high school years. Science includes the humanities, and the humanities include science."[4] Using literature to teach any curriculum-related material is becoming more and more common in education today, as evidenced by many of the teaching strategies used by educators. The whole language approach has its roots in literature. The idea of teaching in thematic units lends itself nicely to using literature across the curriculum.

Because there is a bevy of science curriculum materials on the education market today, the authors examined many curricular programs in order to determine some common objectives. The common thread in all these curriculum materials is their emphasis on an inquiry-based approach to teaching science. In his article, "Science Trade Books and the Educational Market" from the Spring 1988 issue of *Appraisal*, Alfred B. Bortz aptly parallels the importance of literature in science education with its place in an inquiry-based approach to science learning.

> An inquiry-based approach to science education works best because it involves students in a characteristically scientific activity. One might call it the "let's-find-out" approach. Finding out involves observation, experimentation, and research. Finding out brings a sense of wonder and excitement to the learning process and instills in students a drive to be active participants in their own learning . . . . How different that is from single-textbook teaching that treats students as passive recipients of someone else's scientific knowledge! . . . Trade books, in contrast, encourage discovery. Skilled children's science trade book authors appeal to their readers' individual approaches to finding out more about the world. Trade books speak the language of science in individual ways. . . . They are written for finders and are thus invaluable resources for teachers who want to involve their students in finding out.[5]

Although the student objectives given for each section may not exactly parallel a school district's science scope and sequence, *Literature-Based Science* permits teachers the flexibility to select those activities that best fit their students' instructional needs and that foster finding out.

Many activities in the book require small group interaction. Working cooperatively is a tool that will facilitate student learning and scientific investigation. Critical observation skills, which are enhanced by these activities, are absolutely necessary for researchers of any age. A medley of investigative techniques appropriate to each grade level is also utilized. Students are asked to make observations, devise hypotheses, draw conclusions, predict outcomes, categorize and sort data, and compare and interpret results. The authors also attempted to incorporate a variety of projects requiring students to measure and record data, including charting, graphing, individual record keeping, drawing, and diagramming. The activities were designed so that the student is the thinker, the investigator, the researcher, the scientist. This meld between literature and science allows students to view science through their own eyes in the real world and in the world of their imagination. The teacher gives these experiences their shape and validity.

HOW TO USE THIS BOOK AND HOW IT IS ORGANIZED

This book is organized by grade levels: Kindergarten/Transitional/First Grade, Second Grade/Third Grade, and Fourth Grade/Fifth Grade. Each grade level is divided into thematic units: animals, plants, the human body, earth science, space, energy and motion, and ecology. Student objectives are given for each science theme in each grade level. A list of recommended readings, with brief descriptions and notations identifying the objectives they support, follows the objectives. A group introductory activity and an extension activity follow the readings. Next, each section includes a multitude of follow-up activities for the teacher to present to students. All Second Grade/Third Grade and Fourth Grade/Fifth Grade sections contain lists of activities for individual students or small groups of students to implement as independent projects. These activities are addressed to the students and require very little direction from the teacher. The educator is invited to try all of the activities in a given unit at a specific grade level or only those that most closely align with the district scope and sequence. Teachers are also encouraged to review the activities and reading lists in the grade levels both above and below the level of their particular class, since many books and projects are useful and appropriate for more than one grade level.

Concluding each grade level section is a listing of nonprint sources. As the use of technology in education mushrooms, the list and variety of materials for use in curricular areas grow proportionately. Because technology is a tool of science investigation and data collection, the integration of nonprint sources into the science curriculum seems especially appropriate and desirable. The nonprint sources listed are only a few examples of the many products available on the market today. The teacher may choose to introduce them to the class as a whole or use them with a small group of students. Several of the sources listed come with guides that suggest appropriate classroom uses. The blend of print literature and nonprint sources will broaden children's perspectives by allowing them to discover that science is everywhere.

The ideal method of presenting the activities in this book is using a cooperative effort between the person teaching science and the library media specialist. This partnership fosters each project's success by allowing the planners' enthusiasm to build as planning takes place and by permitting shared responsibility for the task's implementation. However, because schools are structured in different ways, *Literature-Based Science* allows either the science teacher, the elementary classroom teacher, or the library media specialist to present the activities. Most school libraries will not have all of the books in this volume. If possible, teachers and library media specialists should use public libraries or interlibrary loan as resources for books. The library media specialist might be willing to buy selections mentioned in this book. Teachers can often apply for small grants to a local foundation or civic group to help fund books for special projects.

A NOTE ON WRITING FOR NONREADERS

Many of the activities in *Literature-Based Science* encourage student writing at a young age. Students can generate language for writing from their experiences. The experiences that young children talk about are related to what they observe or do. Because all of the activities in this book require students to do or observe something, these lessons become the perfect vehicle for language expression. If students are not yet able to write, allow them to draw pictures that depict their language. An adult volunteer, an older student, or the teacher can write what students say under their pictures. Another approach is to simply permit students to tell the adult or older student what they want written. If students can write, but do not have spelling skills, allow them to write the sounds as they hear them.

REFERENCES

1.   Fort, Deborah C. "Science Shy, Science Savvy, Science Smart." *Phi Delta Kappan*, May 1993, p. 678.
2.   Fort, p. 674.
3.   America 2000: An Education Strategy. U.S. Department of Education, 1991.
4.   Fort, p. 678.
5.   Bortz, Alfred B. "Science Trade Books and the Educational Market." *Appraisal*, Spring 1988, p. 5.

CHAPTER

Kindergarten/Transitional/ First Grade

■

LIFE SCIENCE—ANIMALS

STUDENT OBJECTIVES

1. Describe the basic needs of animals.
2. Describe various characteristics of animals.
3. Describe a variety of animal habitats.
4. Classify animals into the following categories: pets, wild, and farm.

RECOMMENDED READINGS

Adams, Georgie. *Fish Fish Fish.* Illustrated by Brigitte Willgoss. Dial Books for Younger Readers, 1992. (Objectives 1, 2, & 3)
Colorful fish take the reader for a swim.

Arnosky, Jim. *Come Out, Muskrats.* Lothrop, Lee and Shepard, 1989. (Objectives 1 & 3)
This simple story explains the playful habits of a family of muskrats.

————. *Crinkleroot's 25 Mammals Every Child Should Know.* Bradbury Press, 1994. (Objective 2)
This information picture book begins by giving the characteristics of mammals and then shows the name and an illustration of many mammals.

————. *Crinkleroot's 25 More Animals Every Child Should Know.* Bradbury Press, 1994. (Objective 2)
This information picture book begins by explaining that animals live in many places and then shows the name and an illustration of a wide variety of animals.

————. *Otters Under Water.* G.P. Putnam's Sons, 1992. (Objective 3)
This story provides the reader with information not only on otters but also on a variety of underwater creatures.

————. *Raccoons and Ripe Corn.* Lothrop, Lee and Shepard, 1987. (Objectives 1 & 3)
Arnosky's simple text and illustrations describe the nocturnal activities of a raccoon family.

Bare, Colleen Stanley. *Love a Llama.* Cobblehill Books, 1994. (Objective 4)
Bare provides an interesting look into the life of a llama as a farm animal and as a pet.

Brown, Craig. *In the Spring.* Greenwillow Books, 1994. (Objectives 3 & 4)
The birth of many farm animals is heralded as a sure sign of spring.

Calhoun, Mary. *While I Sleep.* Illustrated by Ed Young. Morrow Junior Books, 1992. (Objective 1)
A little girl wonders what happens to the rest of the world as she sleeps.

Carle, Eric. *Eric Carle's Animals, Animals.* Poems compiled by Laura Whipple. Illustrated by Eric Carle. Philomel, 1989. (Objective 2)
This collection of animal poetry provides brief glimpses into the characteristics of a variety of animals.

————. *The Very Hungry Caterpillar.* Philomel, 1981. (Objective 2)
Carle's text and illustrations provide the reader with a fun depiction of a caterpillar's transformation to a butterfly.

Davies, Andrew, and Davies, Diana. *Poonam's Pets.* Illustrated by Paul Dowling. Viking, 1990. (Objective 4)
In Poonam's class, the "Pets Assembly" turns out to contain a few surprises.

Denslow, Sharon Phillips. *Hazel's Circle.* Illustrated by Sharon McGinley-Nally. Four Winds Press, 1992. (Objective 4)
Hazel and her pet rooster visit friends as they sell their eggs.

Fleming, Denise. *In the Small, Small Pond.* Henry Holt and Company, 1993. (Objective 3)
Beautiful illustrations and rhyme depict life in the pond through the changing seasons.

Florian, Douglas. *At the Zoo*. Greenwillow, 1992. (Objective 4)
Florian's rhyming text and colorful illustrations describe a typical day at the zoo.

George, William T., and George, Lindsay Barrett. *Beaver at Long Pond*. Illustrated by Lindsay Barrett George. Greenwillow, 1988. (Objective 3)
The Georges describe the procedures that a beaver goes through to build a lodge.

Giffard, Hannah. *Red Fox on the Move*. Dial, 1992. (Objective 1)
Giffard does an excellent job of illustrating the problems urban growth poses for a family of foxes.

Ginsburg, Mirra. *Asleep, Asleep*. Illustrated by Nancy Tafuri. Greenwillow Books, 1992. (Objective 1)
Ginsburg's simple text and Tafuri's illustrations provide a look into various animals' sleeping habits.

Greenwood, Pamela D. *What About My Goldfish?* Illustrated by Jennifer Plecas. Clarion, 1993. (Objective 4)
A young boy is concerned about how his pets will like living in a new town.

Gwynne, Fred. *Easy to See Why*. Simon & Schuster, 1993. (Objective 4)
Gwynne's illustrations show how people look like their pets.

Lewison, Wendy Cheyette. *Going to Sleep on the Farm*. Illustrated by Juan Wijngaard. Dial, 1992. (Objective 3)
As a father describes to his son how each animal on the farm goes to sleep, the animal is pictured in its habitat.

Oram, Hiawyn. *A Creepy Crawly Song Book*. Music by Carl Davis. Illustrated by Satoshi Kitamura. Farrar, Straus and Giroux, 1993. (Objectives 2 & 3)
This wonderful collection of songs about insects and animals paints a vivid picture for every child.

Paxton, Tom. *The Animals' Lullaby*. Illustrated by Erick Ingraham. Morrow Junior Books, 1993. (Objective 2)
Paxton's animal verses focus on the nighttime habits of the animals.

Polacco, Patricia. *The Bee Tree*. Philomel Books, 1993. (Objectives 2 & 3)
A grandfather tries to teach his granddaughter the value of books by taking her on a bee hunt.

Ryder, Joanne. *Where Butterflies Grow*. Illustrated by Lynne Cherry. Dutton, 1989. (Objective 2)
This book combines delightful text and beautiful illustrations to depict the life of butterflies.

Tafuri, Nancy. *This Is the Farmer*. Greenwillow, 1994. (Objective 4)
Simple rhyming text describes the activities and animals that surround a farmer's life.

Wildsmith, Brian, and Wildsmith, Rebecca. *Look Closer*. Harcourt Brace Jovanovich, 1993. (Objective 3)
A walker describes what he sees on his walk.

————. *Wake Up, Wake Up!* Harcourt Brace Jovanovich, 1993. (Objective 4)
This clever farm book describes the morning noises of the farm.

Wilson, Etta. *Music in the Night*. Illustrated by Robin M. Koontz. Cobblehill, 1993. (Objective 4)
This cute story shows animals' reactions to the moon rising over the farm.

Ziefert, Harriet. *Let's Get a Pet*. Illustrated by Mavis Smith. Viking, 1993. (Objective 4)
A family tries to make an informed decision about purchasing a pet.

GROUP INTRODUCTORY ACTIVITY

Preparing for the Activity: Locate a copy of the Georges' *Beaver at Long Pond*. Have available three large pieces of white paper and markers.

Focus: Before reading, tell students they will need to listen carefully for answers to the following questions:

- What is the beaver looking for in the story?
- Where does the beaver live?
- What unusual things does the beaver do in the story?

Objective: To satisfy the objectives of describing characteristics, habitats, and needs of animals, read *Beaver at Long Pond* to the students. After reading, have one piece of white chart paper for each of the following areas: Behavior, Habitat, and Needs. Then have the class fill in each chart with information learned from the story.

Extending Activity: Divide students into four or five groups. Let each group choose an animal from a given list. Students should be able to find age-appropriate information in the library about animals on this list. Then give each group paper to make a simple fact book about their animal. Assign a parent volunteer or older student to each group to help with locating books, reading, and recording information. One section of the book should include information on the animal's habitat; another section should include information on the animal's behavior, and the next section should include information on the animal's needs. Then allow time for each group to share their finished product with the class.

FOLLOW-UP ACTIVITIES FOR
TEACHER AND STUDENTS TO SHARE

1. Before reading Calhoun's *While I Sleep* and Ginsburg's *Asleep, Asleep,* have students discuss the different needs of animals. They should talk about food, shelter, and rest. Then have students think about where their pets rest. Give each student a white sheet of paper. Have them divide it into four equal parts. In the first section, have them draw a picture of where their pets sleep. Then share both books. Next, instruct students to choose three other animals mentioned in either one of the stories and have them draw pictures showing where these animals sleep. Allow time for students to compare their pictures with the ones that are in the books. Have the class as a group make a list of the variety of places that animals sleep. Ask them to think of other animals that sleep in those places.

2. Before sharing the Davies' *Poonam's Pets,* ask students to bring a picture of their pet or pets to class. Have the class make a graph that shows the variety and quantity of pets living with each student. Explain to the students that, in this story about Poonam, they are going to recognize some of the pets as the same as ones included on their graph and others as very different. After reading the story, have students put a check mark by animals on their graph that were also mentioned in the story and make a list of animals that were not included on the graph. Then have students discuss what problems they might have with some of the animals that came to the "Pets Assembly" in the story.

3. Before reading Denslow's *Hazel's Circle,* explain to students that this story is about a girl named Hazel and her rooster, Ike. After giving students that small amount of information, ask where they think this story might take place. Then have students list other animals, besides the rooster, that might be found in the country. As the students brainstorm their ideas, write them on a large cut out of a barn. After reading the story, have students add animals mentioned in the story to their list. Have students continue to add to the farm animal list throughout their study of animals. You could also plan a field trip to a local farm or fairgrounds, adding to the farm animal list. If these field trip locations are not accessible, a local zoo might be an alternative. At the zoo, focus on farm animals. When your list is complete, have students choose one of the animals that they would like to make with construction paper and various other materials. Glue these figures under the appropriate name of the animal on the word barn.

4. Before going on a trip to the zoo, have students list animals that they think they will see. Then read Florian's *At the Zoo.* Ask students if any animals in Florian's book are not at your local zoo. After the class trip to the zoo, reread Florian's book and write down any animals not seen on

your zoo trip. Then have students work with a partner to make a list of 10 of their favorite zoo animals. Each pair should write and illustrate their own book from their list, using Florian's book as an example. He uses two-word, rhyming sentences, e.g., "Hippos float. Mountain goat." The teacher or a parent volunteer may need to write the students' words on their paper. Compile the pages into a book and share with the class.

5. Prior to reading Arnosky's *Come Out, Muskrats* and *Raccoons and Ripe Corn*, ask students if they have ever seen a muskrat or raccoon. Show students pictures of both animals in their habitats. Next, share Arnosky's books. Then, using a large tablet or the chalkboard, make a chart comparing the two. Ask questions that guide students in making comparisons. Where did the muskrats go at night? Where did the raccoons go at night? What foods did each animal eat? How did each animal get around?

6. Before reading Arnosky's *Otters Under Water*, tell students to listen and watch for all the animals Arnosky mentions in this book. After reading the book, ask students to name the animals in the story. Write each name across the bottom of a wall-sized piece of blue butcher paper. Then have students make replicas of these animals using construction paper and markers. Students will then attach their animals to the "underwater habitat," the blue butcher paper.

7. After reading Polacco's fun and fast-paced book, *The Bee Tree*, have students act out the bee hunt. A large room, gym, or even outside would be good settings for this activity. Station students on the "path" described in Polacco's book. At the end of the path, have some honey available for students to sample.

8. Before reading Ryder's *Where Butterflies Grow*, have students make butterfly wings using brightly colored tissue paper and a clothespin. Clip the tissue paper in the middle using the clothespin. While reading the story, have students act out each developmental stage of the caterpillar as it changes into the butterfly. Students will creep, balance, climb, grow, eat, rest, stretch, drift, and fly. When the butterfly is ready to spread its wings and fly, allow the students to use the butterflies they made to show how butterflies soar. Read Carle's *The Very Hungry Caterpillar* as a follow-up to this activity. To allow students to observe the stages of butterfly development, grow butterfly larvae in the classroom.

9. After reading Lewison's *Going to Sleep on the Farm*, have students act out the sleeping behavior of the animal characters in the book. Students may want to add some other animals that were mentioned in Calhoun's *While I Sleep* and Ginsburg's *Asleep, Asleep*.

10. After reading Giffard's *Red Fox on the Move*, have students help make a timeline of the events that lead up to the Fox family finding their new home. Write their ideas for the timeline on a chalkboard. Then allow

students to choose a part of the timeline they would like to illustrate. After they have illustrated and copied a simple sentence to go with their section of the timeline, discuss what other animals might have to move. Also ask students if there are other places in the community where changes are taking place that might affect animals.

11. Read Fleming's *In the Small, Small Pond* to students. After reading, explain to students that the animals mentioned in this story live in a habitat called "a pond." Give examples of other habitats. Some ideas might include the forest, the ocean, the farm, or the desert. Have the class select one habitat. Have students generate a list of animals that live in the habitat and write these animals on the board. Have each student pick an animal. The teacher should also choose an animal. Using construction paper, show students how to tear the paper to create the animal. An example might be an octopus. Simply select a pink or peach-colored piece of construction paper and tear eight tentacles shaped like irregular strips and a body shaped like a rounded oval. Next, glue the tentacles to the body. Glue your octopus to a piece of heavy white paper and color in the water. Add your caption: "An octopus glides." Tell students this demonstration shows how a page can be developed for their classroom book. Have students create their pages in a similar fashion. Explain to students that the pages of the book should show all the animals in their habitat and will be put together to create a book on the habitat selected by the class. The teacher may have to write the captions on the paper for the students. Bind the finished book and display it in the classroom. Students enjoy reading their own work over and over.

12. Share Adams' *Fish Fish Fish* with students. Ask students if fish can be a variety of colors. Be prepared to share photographs or video images of fish with students. Ask students if they have fish at home. If so, invite them to share how these pets are cared for at their house and where their fish live. Using Adams' book as a model, demonstrate how to make a torn construction paper collage fish. Have each student create a fish. After students have made their fish, instruct them to also make pebbles and plant life. Attach a large mural-size piece of white kraft paper to a classroom wall. The students may paint the kraft paper blue using tempera or water colors. Have students use their fish, pebbles, and plant life to make a giant underwater mural.

13. This activity would be a fun culminating activity for a unit on animals or insects. Ask the music teacher in your school or a musically inclined parent to assist with this activity. A piano or guitar would make this activity more exciting for students. Select one of the short, repetitive songs from Oram's *A Creepy Crawly Song Book* to teach to students. Share the music and illustrations with the students and teach them the song. After

they learn the song, ask students to create body movements to accompany the lyrics. Each student could be responsible for one line. Have each student teach their movement to the others. Rehearse several times. Students could also create simple costumes for the insects or animals using construction paper, tape, glue, and crayons. For example, insect antennae can be made from strips of two-inch-wide paper fastened to fit each child's head. Strips of heavy black paper could be glued on to form the antennae. Paint especially designed for use on children's faces can be used to transform a child's face to a buggy face. Students could perform their songs for other classes.

14. Prior to this activity, list all the animals mentioned in Brown's *In the Spring* on the chalkboard. Share Brown's book with students. After the children have listened, ask them to give the baby name for each of the animals on the chalkboard. Ask students to think of another place where lots of different animals might live. Responses might include the zoo, the forest, the ocean, or a pond. Explain to students that the class is going to create a book like Brown's about one of these places. Ask them to select a place. After the place has been selected, have the students list the names of as many animals as possible that could be found in the place. Assign each pair of students an animal from those listed. Explain that the teacher will help them find the name of babies for that type of animal. Allow students to work in pairs to search for a picture of their animal in old magazines. Have students cut out the picture and glue it to heavy paper or cardstock. The teacher or the students can print the name of the animal and the name for its babies on the paper. The pages should be put together in book fashion for students to read at their leisure.

15. Prior to reading Arnosky's *Crinkleroot's 25 Mammals Every Child Should Know* and *Crinkleroot's 25 More Animals Every Child Should Know*, attach a huge piece of mural-size white butcher paper to a wall. Divide the paper into sections entitled Zoo, Farm, Pond, Ocean, Forest, Prairie, Backyard, and By a River. While sharing both of Arnosky's books, have students tell where to place each animal. Write the names of the animals under the proper heading. Some animals will fit into several habitats.

16. Share several selections and illustrations from *Eric Carle's Animals, Animals* with students. After each selection, discuss what characteristic they learned about that animal from the poem and illustration. Have students select one animal they would like to reproduce using a tissue paper collage method similar to Carle's. Students will need tissue paper, glue, white paper, and scissors. Display these pictures in the classroom. Students could copy the accompanying poem to go with their illustration.

17. Before sharing Bare's *Love a Llama*, ask students to vote on how they believe a llama should be classified: pet, wild, or farm animal. Then share Bare's book. Have the students vote again and then ask them the following questions:

    - What made you change your mind?
    - What information made you keep your vote the same?

    Put a huge cut out of a llama on the board. Throughout the day, allow students time to record one fact about the llama on the cut out. At the end of the day, share all the new llama facts.

18. Before sharing Gwynne's *Easy to See Why*, ask students to bring a picture of their pet from home or a picture of a pet they would like to have cut out from a magazine. Then share Gwynne's book. After sharing, have students prepare portraits of their animals and themselves looking somewhat similar. Some pets, like birds and fish, might be particularly interesting.

19. After sharing Greenwood's *What About My Goldfish?*, ask students to bring to class a picture of their pet or a pet they would like to have. Have each student share any special precautions they would need to take if they were moving to a new state with their pet. Then have students share the name of their pet and how their pet got its name. Students could paste the picture of their pet onto a piece of paper and write or dictate a story about how their pet got its name. Share their stories with the class.

20. Share Tafuri's *This Is the Farmer* with students. Explain to students that they are going to act out the rhyme as the class recites it. Give each student the name of one character or animal: farmer, wife, dog, cat, mouse, geese, donkey, and cow. A field trip to a local farm would be fun. After the field trip, students could make up a similar rhyme using all the animals seen on the field trip.

21. Before sharing Paxton's *The Animals' Lullaby*, solicit the help of the music teacher or a musically inclined parent. Teach the lullaby to the students. After they have practiced, allow time for acting out the verses using gestures. When the class has practiced putting the words with the gestures, perform the lullaby for another class or parents.

22. Before sharing Wilson's *Music in the Night*, write the following animal names on the board: Dog, Cow, Dove, Hen, Duck, Horse, and Cat. Provide each student with a 5" x 8" white index card and crayons. Tell the students to draw the animal of their choice from the list on the board. Instruct students to bring their pictures when they gather together to

hear the story. Tell students that as they listen to the story they will hear the name of the animal they are holding. Each time they hear the name of their animal they will need to make the animal noise. Then share Wilson's book. Now do the same activity using the Wildsmiths' *Wake Up, Wake Up!* The animals in the Wildsmiths' book include Dog, Cow, Pig, Goat, Goose, Rooster, and Sheep.

23. After sharing the Wildsmiths' *Look Closer*, have students list the different things the walker saw on his walk. On the list, include what he saw and where he saw it. Then take students on a walk around the neighborhood. As students walk, they should look closely for animals and insects. When students find an animal or insect, stop for a moment and take note of where the animal is and quickly ask the students if they think that is the animal's home or if the animal is out of its home. Discuss what the animal is doing and why the animal is where it is. After the walk, come back to the classroom and add to the list.

24. Before sharing Ziefert's *Let's Get a Pet,* have students discuss their pet, the responsibilities they have in taking care of their pet, and where they got their pet. Next, share Ziefert's book except for the last page. Before sharing the last page, have students write down or draw a picture of the pet they think the family ended up with. Then have them bring their guesses back to the group. Make a list of their answers on the board. Then share the last page of the story.

■

LIFE SCIENCE—PLANTS

STUDENT OBJECTIVES

1. Identify different plants.
2. Describe how plants grow and change.
3. Describe a variety of uses for plants.

RECOMMENDED READINGS

Bunting, Eve. *Flower Garden.* Illustrated by Kathryn Hewitt. Harcourt Brace & Company, 1994. (Objective 2)
    A young girl creates a garden window box as a surprise for her mother.

Carle, Eric. *The Tiny Seed.* Picture Book Studio, 1987. (Objective 2)
A tiny seed survives many obstacles to become a flower.

Ehlert, Lois. *Eating the Alphabet.* Harcourt Brace Jovanovich, 1989. (Objective 1)
Fruits and vegetables from A to Z are listed in this colorful book.

————. *Growing Vegetable Soup.* Harcourt Brace Jovanovich, 1987. (Objective 3)
The ingredients for vegetable soup are planted, grown, picked, and cooked in this bright picture book.

Fleming, Denise. *Lunch.* Henry Holt and Company, 1992. (Objective 1)
This colorful picture book follows a mouse through his huge lunch.

Howard, Ellen. *The Big Seed.* Illustrated by Lillian Hoban. Simon & Schuster, 1993. (Objective 2)
The smallest girl in the class grows the largest plant in the class.

Jordan, Helene J. *How a Seed Grows.* Illustrated by Loretta Krupinski. (Objectives 1 & 2)
This nonfiction book provides a variety of activities to do with seeds.

Krauss, Ruth. *The Carrot Seed.* Illustrated by Crockett Johnson. Harper and Row, 1945. (Objective 2)
A young boy plants a carrot seed and watches it grow.

Lobel, Anita. *Alison's Zinnia.* Greenwillow, 1990. (Objective 1)
Lobel has written and illustrated a gorgeous flower book.

Lobel, Arnold. *The Rose in My Garden.* Illustrated by Anita Lobel. Greenwillow, 1984. (Objectives 1 & 2)
The author plants a beautiful flower garden using a rhyming format.

McMillan, Bruce. *Growing Colors.* Lothrop, Lee & Shepard, 1988. (Objective 1)
This color book depicts a variety of fruits and vegetables.

Reich, Janet. *Gus and the Green Thing.* Walker and Company, 1993. (Objective 2)
A city dog learns about green plants.

Robbins, Ken. *A Flower Grows.* Dial, 1990. (Objectives 1 & 2)
Beautiful illustrations depict the life of an amaryllis.

Rockwell, Anne, and Rockwell, Harlow. *How My Garden Grew.* Macmillan, 1982. (Objective 2)
This simple story outlines the steps needed to plant and care for a garden.

Ryder, Joanne. *Hello, Tree!* Illustrated by Michael Hays. Dutton Children's
Books, 1991. (Objective 3)
This beautifully illustrated book provides delightful descriptions of trees.

Tresselt, Alvin. *The Gift of the Tree.* Illustrated by Henri Sorensen. Lothrop,
Lee & Shepard, 1992. (Objectives 2 & 3)
This story describes a tree's gifts to many different animals.

Udry, Janice May. *A Tree Is Nice.* Illustrated by Marc Simont. Harper and
Row, 1956. (Objective 3)
Many reasons are given explaining why a tree is nice.

GROUP INTRODUCTORY ACTIVITY

Preparing for the Activity: Locate a copy of Tresselt's *The Gift of the Tree.* If
at all possible, take students outside and sit under a tree to read this story.
Upon returning to class, have available two large pieces of chart paper and
markers.
Focus: Before reading, tell students to listen carefully for all the animals that
were helped by the tree and all the ways that nature affected the tree. After
sharing Tresselt's book, title one piece of chart paper "What the Animals
Received from the Tree." Have students list the animals that were helped and
how they were helped. Give students an example, such as, "The tree gave the
squirrels acorns to eat." After students have finished this list, title the other
chart paper "Effects of Nature on the Tree." Have students list what nature
did to the tree throughout the years. An example to share with students
might be, "A winter storm broke off one of the tree limbs."
Objective: To satisfy the objectives of describing how plants grow and change
and the variety of uses of plants, have students choose one of the animals
they listed on the chart. Then have them draw a picture of that animal's
interaction with the tree. Allow time for students to share their pictures with
the class.
Extending Activity: Arrange for students to visit a local forest, nursery, or
tree farm. Have the tour guide discuss with students the importance of trees
in the environment and the importance of planting new trees. This would be
a great activity to do near Arbor Day.

FOLLOW-UP ACTIVITIES FOR
TEACHER AND STUDENTS TO SHARE

Many activities in this section involve tasting a variety of foods. Be sure to
determine which students have food allergies.

  1. Have the following materials available for each student: a 5- to 8-oz.
     clear plastic cup, soil, and a bag of pinto beans. Before reading Jordan's

How A Seed Grows, ask students to bring a seed from home. Be sure to give them some examples, including lima bean, pumpkin, sunflower, watermelon, orange, lemon, or dill seeds. Have each student show the seed they brought and tell how it is used. Share Jordan's book with students. Now have students plant three or four pinto beans in their clear cups. Help students place their beans in the soil so that the beans can be seen around the sides of the cup. Each day have students fill in a simple chart illustrating bean growth. Culminate this activity by reading Krauss' *The Carrot Seed*.

2. Read Ehlert's *Growing Vegetable Soup* to students. Then have students bring their favorite vegetable from home. Make sure they bring a fresh vegetable (not frozen or canned). On a chart add the name of each vegetable brought by students. Have students identify where this vegetable grows—underground or above ground. Add this information to the chart. Now ask students to determine if the vegetable is the root, stalk, leaf, flower, or fruit of the plant. This information should also be added to the chart. Adapt the soup recipe in the back of the book to include all the vegetables brought by students. Have a tasting party. Finally, ask students to use the information on the chart to think of a fun name for their soup creation.

3. After reading Ehlert's *Eating the Alphabet*, arrange to take a trip to a local grocery or farmer's market. Prior to the field trip, give each student a letter of the alphabet printed on a 3" x 5" index card. Explain to students that their task will be to find a fruit or vegetable beginning with the letter on their card. At the market, allow students to purchase a fruit or vegetable beginning with their letter. After returning to the classroom, have each student identify the name of the vegetable or fruit that they purchased. As students identify their purchases, have the class determine if the food is the root, stalk, leaf, flower, or fruit of the plant. Finally, allow students to taste the fruits and vegetables.

4. The timing of this activity should be coordinated with the local planting season. Enlist help from parent volunteers to prepare for a class garden. Parents can prepare the soil in a small corner of the playground. Share *How My Garden Grew* by Anne and Harlow Rockwell. Create a list of what is needed to plant a garden. Invite parents to send a seed or bulb from home for their child to plant. Be sure to have parents identify the seed or bulb. Have extra seeds and bulbs available. Using bulb and seed catalogs, have students cut out a picture that shows the plants to be planted. Attach these pictures to 3" x 5" cards and then attach the cards to wooden sticks. Allow students to plant their bulb or seed and mark its place in the garden. Each day, visit the garden to observe its progress and to water as necessary.

5. After sharing Lobel's *Alison's Zinnia*, provide students with plant and flower catalogs, construction paper, crayons, glue, and scissors. Assign each child a letter of the alphabet. Explain that they will be making a class flower alphabet book. Students should cut out a picture of the blossom of a plant beginning with their assigned alphabet letter. After pasting the picture on their paper, the students should draw in the stems and leaves. Next print the name of the plant on the paper. Laminate the paper and bind it into a class book.

6. Purchase an amaryllis bulb for this activity. Share Robbins' *A Flower Grows* with students. Use Robbins' precise instructions given in the back of the book to plant a class amaryllis. As a class, measure the growth of the plant daily. Discuss the changes that students observe each day. Make a simple class bar graph depicting the daily growth of the plant.

7. After reading Carle's *The Tiny Seed*, have students generate a list to be recorded on the chalkboard of all the things that made it impossible for the seeds to become plants. Keep this list on the chalkboard. Next have students list what happened to some of the plants. After making and discussing these lists, have students add other problems that seeds and plants might have. Read Carle's book a second time, having students play the parts of seeds and plants. Some students will need to be assigned the parts of the sun, bird, mouse, ocean, desert, child, boy, and girl. After practicing their roles, students can present the story to other classrooms.

8. Before reading Lobel's *The Rose in My Garden*, have scissors, flower catalogs, pieces of white poster board, and paste available for students. Write the names of the following flowers on small pieces of paper: roses, hollyhocks, marigolds, zinnias, daisies, bluebells, lilies, peonies, pansies, tulips, and sunflowers. Give each student the name of one flower. Instruct students to find their flower in the catalog, cut it out, paste it on the white piece of posterboard, and write the name of the flower below it. Next tell students to bring their flowers and come listen to a story. Tell them to listen carefully for the name of the flower they are holding. Explain to students that everytime they hear the name of their flower they are to hold up their posterboard high in the air. Next, read Lobel's book. While the teacher is reading, students should be holding up their flowers at the appropriate time. When the story is finished, ask students to tell which flowers they thought were the prettiest, the tallest, the brightest, the most colorful, the biggest, and the tiniest.

9. Before reading Udry's Caldecott Award winner, *A Tree Is Nice*, ask students the following questions:

- If you were a bird, why would you think a tree is nice?
- If you were a squirrel, why would you think a tree is nice?

- If you were a cow, why would you think a tree is nice?
- If you were a cat being chased by a dog, why would you think a tree is nice?

Then tell students to think about why they, as a boy or girl, think a tree is nice. List their answers on the chalkboard. Next, read Udry's book. Compare the list on the board with the reasons Udry gives in her book. Add to the list on the board if necessary. Next, have a huge cut out of a tree attached to the bulletin board. Provide students with various colors of construction paper, markers, scissors, and glue. Tell students that each of them will be adding a picture to the giant tree cut out, depicting why they think a tree is nice. Following the simple directions near the end of Udry's book, provide an opportunity for students to plant a tree on the playground.

10. Prior to this activity, assemble the following materials: soil, small clay flower pots, seeds, tempera paint, sponges, and small rocks or pebbles. Share Bunting's *Flower Garden* with students. Explain to the students that each of them will make a flower pot garden for their mother or grandmother. Cut sponges to desired shapes. Hearts, stars, and flowers are easy shapes to cut. Each student should dip the sponge in tempera and paint her or his flower pot. Allow flower pots to dry before planting. Instruct students to put pebbles or small rocks in their pot to cover the bottom. Next, have students fill the pot with soil and plant the seeds. Finally, have students water their plants and place the pots in a window. Water as needed. The teacher should place a large piece of white paper on the wall near the plant to make a class "breaking ground" chart. Put each student's name down the left side of the chart and the dates across the bottom. Put a mark on the corresponding date as each student's plant emerges from the soil. The students can also keep their own growth diaries by documenting each day's growth with a simple line drawing showing the growth of their plants. Plants could be given to mothers or grandmothers for Mother's Day or Valentine's Day.

11. After sharing McMillan's *Growing Colors* with students, take a field trip to a local grocery store or farmer's market. Before departing on the field trip, give each student a small piece of colored paper. Be sure to use each color in McMillan's book. Tell students that they will need to find a fruit or vegetable that matches their color. After the field trip, ask students to share the name of their fruit or vegetable with the class.

12. Before sharing Reich's *Gus and the Green Thing*, ask students what color they think of when they think of plants, trees, and grass. Share the title of the story and ask students what they think the green thing might be. Share Gus' story. After the reading, have students write an ending to the

story that includes how Gus would have to take care of the plant he found. Give younger students a piece of white 8½" x 11" paper and instruct them to fold the paper in half. Then have them draw two pictures depicting what Gus would need to do to take care of the plant. Display their work in the classroom.

13. Before sharing Ryder's *Hello, Tree!* with students, make a huge cut out of a tree using kraft paper. Make sure to cut branches, leaves, and roots to put on the tree. Put this tree on a bulletin board and then gather students around the board to listen to the story. Instruct students to listen carefully for words that describe the tree. After sharing the story, tell students that they will be helping to describe the tree on the bulletin board. Begin by looking at the branches and limbs. Ask students how the branches and limbs were described in the story and how they were used in the story. As students respond, write their answers on a branch or limb of the tree. As each part of the tree is completed, reread the parts of Ryder's book pertaining to that particular part. Do the same for each part of the tree.

14. While sharing Fleming's *Lunch*, allow time for students to guess what the mouse is eating before turning the page. After sharing Fleming's book, provide each student with a 3" x 5" index card. On each index card, write the name of a color and provide a sample of that color drawn on the card with crayon or marker. Begin by using the colors in the book, although blue might be difficult to use in this activity. Then provide students with magazines and scissors. Allow time for students to cut out a picture of a food that matches their color card. Instruct students to paste their picture on an 8½" x 11" sheet of paper. Have parent volunteers or older children help students dictate two words that describe their food. One of the words should be a color word, the other a word to describe the food. Give examples from the book. When students have completed their pages, compile their work in a book format. Tell students that the title of their book will be "Dinner." Begin sharing by using the words on the first page of Fleming's book, then use the students' words and pictures. At the conclusion of the book, use the words on Fleming's back pages. At the end, say "breakfast" instead of "dinnertime."

15. Prior to this activity, ask students to save and rinse their milk cartons from the cafeteria. Have students cut the tops off the milk cartons. Read Howard's *The Big Seed* to students. After reading, allow each student to choose a seed to plant from a variety of types. Plant the seeds in soil in the milk cartons. Take care of the seeds by having students model the methods used by students in Howard's book: water when the soil is dry, rotate in the window so the plants will grow straight, etc. Ask the class to determine which student had the biggest seed, the smallest seed, the round-

est seed, the flattest seed, the darkest seed, and the lightest seed. Allow the students to take the seedlings home to plant in their outdoor gardens.

■

HUMAN BODY

STUDENT OBJECTIVES

1. Identify the body organ associated with each of the five senses.
2. Study the importance of exercise.
3. Describe the basic needs of humans.
4. Discuss proper care of the body.

RECOMMENDED READINGS

Agell, Charlotte. *Dancing Feet.* Harcourt Brace & Company, 1994. (Objective 4)
Agell describes various parts of the body and their uses in a simple, rhyming format.

Baer, Edith. *The Wonder of Hands.* Photographs by Tana Hoban. Macmillan, New York, 1992. (Objective 1)
Hoban's beautiful black-and-white photos are paired with Baer's simple rhyme to create a beautiful book about hands.

Brandenberg, Aliki. *I'm Growing.* HarperCollins, 1992. (Objective 4)
A little boy tells of growing up and changing.

————. *My Feet.* Thomas Y. Crowell, 1990. (Objective 1)
Aliki's simple text and illustrations provide information on feet and the many different ways feet are used.

————. *My Five Senses.* HarperCollins, 1989. (Objective 1)
A boy describes his adventures with each of his senses.

————. *My Hands.* Thomas Y. Crowell, 1990. (Objective 1)
Aliki's simple text and illustrations provide information on parts of the hand and the many different ways hands are used.

Brown, Marc. *Arthur's Chicken Pox.* Little, Brown & Company, 1994. (Objectives 3 & 4)

Arthur's plans to attend the circus are spoiled when he comes down with the chicken pox.

Collis, Annabel. *You Can't Catch Me!* Little, Brown and Company, 1993. (Objectives 2, 3, & 4)
A little boy takes the reader on a tour of his playground.

Dodds, Dayle Ann. *Do Bunnies Talk?* Illustrated by A. Dubanevich. HarperCollins, 1992. (Objective 1)
Dubanevich's bright artwork combines with Dodd's text to provide lots of listening interest.

Guthrie, Woody, with Guthrie, Marjorie Mazia. *Woody's 20 Grow Big Songs: Songs and Pictures.* HarperCollins, 1992. (Objective 4)
A collection of fun, simple songs that will help children learn about their bodies.

Kuklin, Susan. *When I See My Dentist.* . . . Bradbury Press, 1988. (Objectives 3 & 4)
Photographs document a child's visit to the dentist.

————. *When I See My Doctor.* . . . Bradbury Press, 1988. (Objectives 2 & 3)
Photographs document a child's visit to the doctor.

Kuskin, Karla. *Soap Soup and Other Verses.* HarperCollins, 1992. (Objective 4)
This group of poems vividly describes a variety of bodily functions.

Macdonald, Maryann. *Rosie's Baby Tooth.* Illustrated by Melissa Sweet. Atheneum, 1991. (Objective 4)
Rosie must decide between her tooth and the tooth fairy.

Rockwell, Harlow. *My Dentist.* William Morrow Company, Inc., 1987. (Objectives 3 & 4)
Rockwell's simple text and drawings describe a child's view of her visit to the dentist.

Showers, Paul. *Ears Are for Hearing.* Illustrated by Holly Keller. HarperTrophy, 1990. (Objective 1)
Simple text describes the function of the ear and how it works.

————. *Look at Your Eyes.* Illustrated by True Kelley. HarperCollins, 1992. (Objectives 1 & 4)
A young child describes eyes and their characteristics, parts, and functions.

Walsh, Ellen Stoll. *Hop Jump*. Harcourt Brace & Company, 1993. (Objective 2)

A single frog decides to try dancing instead of hopping, and soon all the other frogs join him.

GROUP INTRODUCTORY ACTIVITY

Preparing for the Activity: Begin by asking students to help list the five senses on the chalkboard. After writing the names of each of the senses across the top of the chalkboard, explain to students that each of the senses is used many times during the day. After each classroom activity, have students tell which senses were used to do that activity. For example, when the students come back from lunch have them write "Lunch" under each of the senses they used. Continue to add to the list throughout the day. At the end of the day, tell students that they will use the list the following day as well.

Focus: The day after making this list, tell students that they will be listening to a story about one little boy's experiences with his five senses. Read Aliki's *My Five Senses*. As Aliki introduces each of the five senses, have pairs of students think of one way that each sense is used. Allow time for students to share their ideas with the rest of the class. After reading the book, have students work with their neighbor to decide on one activity that incorporates more than one of the senses. Have each pair of students share their activity with the class and identify which senses they used for their particular activity. For example, one pair of students might select eating a banana, which involves both tasting and touching, as their activity to share with the class.

Objective: To satisfy the objective of identifying the body organ associated with each of the five senses, allow the class to create a body rhyme. Students should include the senses and the appropriate body part and function by using words and body movements.

Extending Activity: Provide each student with a piece of white typing paper. Have them fold the paper into four equal parts. Instruct students to choose four of the five senses. After they have made their decision, have them title each square of their paper with the name of one of the senses they chose. In each square, have them draw a picture that shows something they might do using that sense. Provide students with another piece of paper that they will fold in half. Instruct students to write down two senses on each half of the paper. Then have students draw a picture of an activity that requires them to use both senses. For example, students who wrote "smelling" and "tasting" on one side of their paper might choose to draw a picture of someone eating a peach.

FOLLOW-UP ACTIVITIES FOR
TEACHER AND STUDENTS TO SHARE

1. Provide students with paper and pencils. Allow pairs of students to trace
    one another's hands. When students come back together as a group, make
    a list on the chalkboard of all the different ways they use their hands.
    Before reading Baer's *The Wonder of Hands*, instruct students to hold up
    one of their traced hands each time something is mentioned that was
    included on the class list. Then share Baer's book. After students have
    studied the other senses, have them work in four small groups to develop
    books similar to Baer's *The Wonder of Hands* for eyes, nose, mouth, and
    ears.

2. Before reading Aliki's *My Hands*, have students brainstorm all the differ-
    ent ways they use their hands and write their ideas on a large piece of
    chart paper. After reading, add to the list. For homework, assign students
    to trace the hands of each of member of their family and ask them to
    bring their hands to class. Make mobiles of each family's hands. Another
    activity would be to use overlapping cut outs of students' hands to make
    a bulletin board border.

3. Before reading Rockwell's *My Dentist*, print the following words on the
    chalkboard: drill, x-ray machine, mirror, tartar, round brush, rinse, spit,
    rubber buffer, polish, and cavities. Use a large piece of kraft paper to cover
    the list of words. Explain to students that they are going to guess what the
    story they are about to hear is about. They will guess by looking at a list of
    words that are in the story. Uncover one word at a time and allow two or
    three children to guess what they think the story is about by looking at
    that word. As students guess, write their guesses beside each word. By the
    time the word "cavities" is uncovered, most students should have guessed
    that the book is about going to the dentist. Then read Rockwell's book.
    After the reading, have students look at the list of words again, this time
    to list the words in the order they appeared in the story. When the words
    are correctly ordered, have the class come up with a simple sentence that
    explains how each word relates to going to the dentist. Allow students to
    add any other sentences that they feel are important to a visit to the
    dentist. Ask a local dentist to come visit the classroom and show the
    tools that he or she uses. Also have the dentist demonstrate proper brush-
    ing techniques. Prepare a Class Brushing Chart with each child's name,
    date, and columns titled "Morning" and "Evening." Instruct students to
    put a check mark beside their name each morning, indicating whether or
    not they brushed after dinner and after breakfast. Keep this chart for two
    weeks and discuss chart results with the class at the end of that period.

4. The first day a student loses a tooth or comes to class with a tooth missing, read Macdonald's *Rosie's Baby Tooth* to the class. Keep a huge cut out of a tooth on a chalkboard or wall. As students lose their teeth, have them add their name and how they lost their tooth to the cut out. Begin by adding Rosie's name and what made her tooth come out.

5. Before reading Kuklin's *When I See My Dentist. . .*, provide each student with a sheet of white paper. Tell the class to draw a picture of one instrument that dentists use when they give children a checkup. Allow students time to draw and color their pictures. As they finish, go around and label their pictures with the name of the instrument they have drawn. Allow students to provide the name. Gather students together in a group and provide time for each student to share her or his drawing. Then read Kuklin's book. Have students go back to their desks and add the correct name of their instrument to their paper. If there are instruments discussed in the book that students have not drawn, allow them an opportunity to make new drawings. Collect the students' pictures and make them into a classroom book. After sharing this story, invite a local dentist to come visit the class. Have students prepare interview questions prior to the visit.

6. Before reading Showers' *Look at Your Eyes*, provide each student with a small mirror. Explain to students that they need to look closely into the mirror. Ask them what they see, and what body part they use to see with. Then have students tell about their eyes:

   - What color are they?
   - What other parts of their face share the word "eye"? [eye brow, eyelash, eyelid]
   - What other things do they see?

   Write their list of answers on the chalkboard. Next, ask students to bring their mirrors and come listen to a story. As the story is read, allow students to look into their mirrors and do some of the activities mentioned in Showers' book. Let them make faces, squint, and watch their pupils change size.

7. Share several of the poems from Kuskin's *Soap Soup and Other Verses*. Ask each student to select her or his favorite poem. Have students determine which body part each poem relates to. Make available to students a variety of old magazines. Instruct students to cut pictures of that body part from magazines. Some of their pictures should show how that body part is clothed in a variety of weather situations; others should show that body part being used in daily activities. Help the students make a classroom

mural with the pictures by covering a classroom wall with white kraft paper. The paper should be divided into body part sections. Have students paste their pictures in the appropriate section of the mural. When the mural is complete, ask students to explain their picture choices.

8. Share Collis' *You Can't Catch Me!* with the students. Ask students to identify the action words in the book: "What things did the boy do on the playground?" List these things on the chalkboard and remind students that all these activities are exercise. Ask students to also make a list of things they do on the school playground. Have each student select his or her favorite playground activity. Provide a variety of materials for students to make simple collages of this activity. Use Collis' book to show a variety of collages to students. Give students heavy paper, glue, and a variety of scraps, including string, twine, ribbon, wallpaper scraps, fabric scraps, lace, cardboard scraps, feathers, and any other readily available items. Display the collages in the school.

9. Before sharing Kuklin's *When I See My Doctor. . .*, ask students to think about the last time they went to visit the doctor. Provide students with 8½" x 11" pieces of white drawing paper and have them draw a picture depicting one part of their experience in the doctor's office. As students tell about the pictures, write down their words on their pictures. Then allow time for students to share their pictures with the class. Display the pictures around the classroom. Prepare cards with pictures of a variety of doctor's tools on them. Write the names of these tools on the back of each card. As each card is held up, ask students if they recognize the instrument. Include pictures of the following: stethoscope, otoscope, flashlight, tongue depressors, reflex hammer, hemoglobinometer, and sphygmomanometer. Then ask if they know the name of the instrument. Explain to students that, in the story, they will be learning the names and uses of these instruments. After reading the story, compare the students' answers to the book's explanations of each tool. After each experience depicted in the story, ask students to compare their illustrations on display with those in the book. This would be a good opportunity to invite a local doctor to share with children the facets of a typical office visit. Ask the doctor to bring some of his or her instruments to show the students.

10. Before reading Dodds' *Do Bunnies Talk?*, tell students that they are going to listen to some noises and try to guess what makes the noises. Stand behind a screen and have the following items prepared for sharing: zipper, drum, clock, cymbals, a balloon to pop, and a twig to snap. When the students have heard all of these noises, ask which sense they used to figure out what made each of the noises. Then share the story with students. Instruct students to bring a paper sack filled with one noise-making item. Tell students that they will be having the other children

guess what is making the noise. After doing this activity, share Showers' *Ears Are for Hearing*. This book gives simple, yet detailed, explanations of how the ear works. Provide students with their own simple illustration of the ear, similar to the one on page 9 of Showers' book. Throughout the sharing of this book, stop and allow time for the students to label their pictures.

11. After reading Aliki's *My Feet*, have students act out the various ways mentioned in the story that feet are used, including walking, running, skipping, marching, kicking, hopping, tiptoeing, skating, and dancing. Provide the students with one huge piece of white kraft paper and a variety of colors of tempera paint. Help students to make one footprint, allowing them to use the color of their choice. Hang the mural in the classroom or hallway. Provide each student with a piece of white construction paper, scissors, and a pencil. Instruct students to trace around one of their feet and cut out the foot. Next, tell students that they will be making a long chart depicting their feet from the smallest to the largest. Begin by asking two students to bring their cut outs to the front of the class. Have them place their cut outs on a long piece of black kraft paper on the floor. Then ask two more students to place their feet in the proper size order with the feet already on the floor. Continue this activity until all of the cut out feet have been placed in order. Then allow each student to glue her or his foot on a long piece of black kraft paper. Display this chart on a classroom wall.

12. Locate Guthrie's *Woody's 20 Grow Big Songs: Songs and Pictures*. Solicit the help of a music teacher to teach the students a variety of the songs in the song book. Ask students to create movements to accompany each selection. Using one of Guthrie's songs to open or close the daily instruction on the human body might be a fun idea.

13. Before reading Walsh's *Hop Jump*, discuss with students the importance of movement and exercise. Explain that the story they will be listening to has lots of moving words. Read through the story once. Then have students list the moving words they heard in the story. Next, ask students who would like to volunteer to act out one of the moving words. As the volunteers act out, have their classmates try to determine which muscles and body parts they are using. Draw a huge outline of a human body on the chalkboard. As parts of the body are mentioned, mark them on the body outline. Then choose one student to be Betsy and ask the other students to be the frogs in the story. Read the story again, allowing time for students to act out as the story is shared. Have the class act out the story for other classrooms or parents.

14. A few days before sharing Aliki's *I'm Growing*, ask the students to bring a photograph of themselves to class. Tell students to bring a baby or pre-

school photograph. Display the photographs on a bulletin board. Just before sharing Aliki's book, gather students around the bulletin board and ask them to guess which photograph belongs to which student. Then allow time for each child to show the picture he or she brought. Next, ask students to name some ways that they have changed since their picture was taken.

- Can they still wear the clothes they had on in the picture?
- Have they learned to do anything new since the picture was taken?
- Have they had another birthday since the picture was taken?
- Have they lost or gained any teeth?

Allow time for students to share their responses. Then share Aliki's book. After sharing, go back to the photographs and ask students if there is anything else they can think of that has changed since the photo was taken. Allow time for discussion.

15. Before sharing Brown's *Arthur's Chicken Pox*, make a photocopy of each child's school picture. Be sure to ask photographer's permission to copy school photographs for this purpose. Give each child a copy of her or his school picture and instruct the class to make polka dots on their pictures if they have had the chicken pox. Then make a graph representing those that have had the chicken pox and those that have not. Next, ask students who have had the chicken pox to tell what they felt helped them get better. It might be oatmeal baths, chicken soup, or medicine. Write their ideas on the board and then share Brown's story. After sharing, ask students how Arthur felt and why they think D.W. wanted to pretend she had the chicken pox. Allow time for students to share their ideas.

16. Read Agell's *Dancing Feet* to students. Next, divide the students into seven groups, one group to represent each of the body parts mentioned in the story. Have a parent volunteer or an older student helper work with each group. After students are sitting in groups, give them a card with the name and picture of their particular body part printed on it. Have students brainstorm all the ways that particular body part can be used. Have the helpers write down their ideas. Tell students they will be making their own book similar to Agell's. Their page of the book should include a picture of their body part and the rhyme that their group created to go with their body part. Remind students about the pattern of the rhymes used in Agell's book. Allow time for students to work on this and then bring them back together as a group. Have each group orally share their portion of the book with the class. Write each sentence on a separate sheet of paper and allow each child in the group to illustrate one of the pages. Bind the book and display it in the classroom or library.

■

EARTH SCIENCE

STUDENT OBJECTIVES

1. Identify the basic components of the earth: land, air, and water.
2. Identify the four seasons.
3. Identify the observable differences in the seasons.
4. Identify how clothing needs change due to seasonal weather.

RECOMMENDED READINGS

Brown, Margaret Wise. *The Summer Noisy Book.* Illustrated by Leonard Weisgard. HarperCollins, 1993. (Objective 3)
This beautiful book describes summer and its many sounds.

Calmenson, Stephanie. *Hotter Than a Hot Dog!* Illustrated by Elivia Savadier. Little, Brown & Company, 1994. (Objective 3)
Delightful story of a little girl and her grandmother who are overwhelmed by the summer heat and head to the beach for relief.

Carlstrom, Nancy White. *How Does the Wind Walk?* Illustrated by Deborah Kogan Ray. Macmillan, 1993. (Objectives 1, 2, & 3)
Beautiful illustrations and simple text describe the role of the wind in each of the four seasons.

———. *What Does the Rain Play?* Illustrated by Henri Sorensen. Macmillan, 1993. (Objective 1)
A boy listens to all the sounds of the rain.

DeWitt, Lynda. *What Will the Weather Be?* Illustrated by Carolyn Croll. HarperCollins, 1991. (Objective 4)
Using simple text, DeWitt provides lots of good information on how weather is predicted.

Dorros, Arthur. *Follow the Water from Brook to Ocean.* HarperCollins, 1991. (Objective 1)
Dorros' simple text clearly describes the many places water is located on Earth.

Fleischman, Susan. *The Boy Who Looked for Spring.* Illustrated by Donna Diamond. Harcourt Brace Jovanovich, 1993. (Objective 3)
A boy answers three riddles to awaken the sleeping Mother Earth for spring.

Fleming, Denise. *In the Small, Small Pond*. Henry Holt and Company, 1993. (Objectives 2 & 3)
Beautiful illustrations and rhyme depict life in the pond through the changing seasons.

George, Jean Craighead. *Dear Rebecca, Winter Is Here*. Illustrated by Loretta Krupinski. HarperCollins, 1993. (Objectives 3 & 4)
The changes winter brings to nature and humans are described by a grandmother.

Goennel, Heidi. *Seasons*. Little, Brown and Company, 1986. (Objectives 3 & 4)
Simple text and delightful illustrations beautifully depict the seasons.

Hest, Amy. *Ruby's Storm*. Illustrated by Nancy Cote. Macmillan, 1994. (Objectives 3 & 4)
Ruby's walk to Grampa's becomes an adventure when a spring storm arrives.

Hirschi, Ron. *Spring*. Photographs by Thomas D. Mangelsen. Cobblehill Books, 1990. (Objectives 2 & 3)
Photographs and simple text depict animals in their habitats during the spring season.

————. *Winter*. Photographs by Thomas D. Mangelsen. Cobblehill Books, 1990. (Objectives 2 & 3)
Photographs and simple text depict animals in their habitats during the winter season.

Kandoian, Ellen. *Molly's Seasons*. Cobblehill, 1992. (Objectives 2, 3, & 4)
This picture book provides simple descriptions and calendars for each season.

Keown, Elizabeth. *Emily's Snowball: The World's Biggest*. Illustrated by Irene Trivas. Atheneum, 1992. (Objectives 3 & 4)
A little girl and her friends create the biggest snowball in the world.

Knutson, Kimberly. *Muddigush*. Macmillan, 1992. (Objective 1)
This clever book describes the sensual adventures of several children playing in the mud.

Maass, Robert. *When Spring Comes*. Henry Holt and Company, 1994. (Objectives 2, 3, & 4)
Colorful photographs and simple text describe the many changes that accompany spring.

————. *When Summer Comes*. Henry Holt and Company, 1993. (Objectives 2, 3, & 4)
Colorful photographs and simple text describe the many changes that accompany summer.

Patron, Susan. *Dark Cloud Strong Breeze*. Illustrated by Peter Catalanotto. Orchard Books, 1994. (Objective 3)
A little girl's father locks his keys in his car just as a rainstorm threatens.

Schweninger, Ann. *Springtime*. Viking, 1993. (Objective 3)
Schweninger describes spring happenings that occur both in nature and in society.

————. *Summertime*. Viking, 1992. (Objective 3)
The author describes summertime happenings that occur both in nature and in society.

Serfozo, Mary. *Rain Talk*. Illustrated by Keiko Narahashi. Macmillan, 1993. (Objective 1)
Serfozo's simple text and Narahashi's watercolor illustrations depict the beauty in a simple summer rainstorm.

Weiss, Nicki. *On a Hot, Hot Day*. G.P. Putnam's Sons, 1992. (Objectives 2, 3, & 4)
A mother and her son enjoy each season together.

Willes, Jeanne. *Earth Weather as Explained by Professor Xargle*. Illustrated by Tony Ross. Dutton, 1993. (Objective 4)
Professor Xargle provides a fascinating account of Earthlet's encounters with weather.

GROUP INTRODUCTORY ACTIVITY

Preparing for the Activity: Locate Kandoian's *Molly's Seasons*. Have four large sheets of kraft paper ready for students. Label each sheet with the name of one of the seasons. Have available to students a variety of old calendars, markers, old magazines, and glue. If you live in an area where distinct lines between seasons are not evident, it is important to show pictures of all seasons to students. Discuss the characteristics of each season.

Focus: Assemble students in a group on the floor. Share the first part of the book that tells all the reasons Molly enjoys the different seasons. After reading this part to students, tell them they will be working with other students on a poster about their favorite season. In four different places around the classroom, place the four sheets of kraft paper, labeled with the names of the seasons. Next, tell students to choose their favorite season and to go to the sheet of paper labeled with that season. Instruct students to cover their papers with anything and everything they want others to know about their season. They will need to include calendar pages showing when their season begins and ends; magazine cut outs of appropriate clothing, foods, and activities; drawings of holidays; and any other information they think is important to their season.

Objective: To satisfy the objectives of identifying and recognizing observable differences and clothing needs of the different seasons, students will share their finished products with other class members. Students might try to convince other students why they think their season is the best. After their presentations, prepare a class graph entitled, "Which Season Is Your Favorite?" This graph will depict the number of students selecting each season as their favorite. Have students discuss the results.

Extending Activity: Finish reading *Molly's Seasons* to the entire class. Show students where New Zealand is on a globe. Then ask students to once again divide into their season groups. Have each group discuss how Ollie's seasons in New Zealand were different than their seasons. Ask them to consider what kinds of things Ollie might be enjoying during their particular season.

FOLLOW-UP ACTIVITIES FOR
TEACHER AND STUDENTS TO SHARE

Because so many books in this section are about the seasons, introducing these books at the appropriate season would be ideal. Summer books may be introduced at the beginning or end of the school year, depending on when school begins and ends.

1. After reading Brown's *The Summer Noisy Book*, have students make an audiocassette tape of the sounds of summer. Begin by asking the students to make a list of the sounds they might hear in the summer. This list could include thunder, frogs, birds, crickets, June bugs, crowd noises at summer ball games, beach sounds, and sounds of outdoor play. Have small groups of children brainstorm ways to create these noises and perform them for the tape.

2. Share Schweninger's *Summertime* with your class. One of the fun activities in this book is making ice pops, which could be eaten on the playground. A field trip to a local fruit and vegetable market would be an appropriate culminating activity for a unit on summer. Before you go on the field trip, have students find out which vegetables and fruits are available during this season. Several of these seasonal fruits and vegetables could be purchased on the field trip and sampled at school.

3. If at all possible, read Keown's *Emily's Snowball: The World's Biggest* to your class on a snowy day. After reading, challenge the other classes in the primary level to a snowball-building contest. If snow is not a possibility in your area, or as an additional activity, have teams of students create snowballs using papier-mâché. Newspaper strips, water, white poster paint, flour, and balloons will be needed for this activity. Use three snowballs to create a papier-mâché snowman. Have students bring a hat, scarf, carrot (nose), nuts (eyes), sticks (arms), and red felt or yarn (mouth) to dress the snowman. Display "snowballs" around your snowman.

4. Before reading George's *Dear Rebecca, Winter Is Here*, ask students to listen for the signs of winter. After reading, list the signs of winter that George identified in the story as the students recall them. Have students bring one sign of winter from home. Bring a package of hot cocoa mix as an example. Let students share their winter items with the class. It might be fun to prepare cocoa for the whole class to set the mood.

5. Before reading Fleischman's *The Boy Who Looked for Spring*, ask students to listen for the answers to the three riddles about spring. Have students list other signs of spring. Record their responses on the board. Have students select one of these signs of spring to use in a poem about spring. Provide each child with a piece of paper that has the beginning four lines of the rhyme from Fleischman's book already written on it. Have students dictate to a teacher or volunteer the final three lines of their spring rhyme.

6. Share Schweninger's *Springtime* with students, then have the students make a timeline filled with spring activities. Start the timeline by marking the first day of spring and end it by marking the last day of spring. Then ask students to fill in other important spring events from Schweninger's book. Students might choose to include April showers, baby animals, outdoor activities, and spring holidays. Students could also do the seed planting activity included in the book.

7. After reading Knutson's *Muddigush*, let students "mud paint" with their hands. Use brown fingerpaint mixed with a small amount of water and dirt, or use chocolate pudding. This activity works best using very large sheets of heavy white paper. Display the mud paintings in the classroom.

8. After reading Carlstrom's *What Does the Rain Play?*, have students imitate the sounds of a hard rain, a soft rain, and thunder using a variety of instruments. For example, clanging cymbals can be thunder and soft drum beats can be the pitter-patter of the rain. Following this activity, read Serfozo's *Rain Talk*. Discuss with students why rain is important for the earth.

9. Before reading DeWitt's *What Will the Weather Be?*, have students cut out pictures of an umbrella, coat, swimsuit, and sweater (or other clothing that they would wear for each season). Then have students sit in a semicircle, placing their cut out pictures on the floor in front of them. As you read the book, stop occasionally and have students show the appropriate article of clothing that would go with the particular weather being discussed.

10. Begin this activity by sharing the introduction to Willes' *Earth Weather as Explained by Professor Xargle*. After reading each of the four sections— too wet, too hot, too windy, and too cold—have students identify what seasons match each of those conditions. Then provide each student with a piece of paper divided into four equal parts. Help students label each

section with the name of a different season and Xargle's description of that season. For example: "Winter—Too Cold." Next, provide students with old magazines, scissors, and paste. Ask students to cut out as many types of clothing as they can find in their magazine. Finally, have students glue their cut outs of clothing to the appropriate section of their paper.

11. After sharing Weiss' *On a Hot, Hot Day*, invite each student to bring her or his favorite piece of clothing from home. Each student should show the favorite item and tell in which season it is worn.

12. Before reading Goennel's *Seasons*, print the names of the seasons on 4" x 6" index cards, laminate the cards, and tape them to the chalkboard. Using Goennel's illustrations for examples, also make simple, laminated cut outs of items characteristic of the seasons. Then read Goennel's book to students. Afterward, choose students to place the seasonal cut outs beside the name of the appropriate season.

13. Before reading Dorros' *Follow the Water from Brook to Ocean*, write the following words on the board: dam, erosion, waterfall, meanders, flood, reservoir, and delta. Pronounce each of these words for the students. Tell students they will need to listen to the story to find out what these words mean. Then read Dorros' book, stopping to discuss each term as it is presented in the book. After finishing the story, provide each student with an envelope containing the following words: rain or snowfall, brook, stream, river, and ocean. Tell students to place these words in the correct order beginning with rain or snow melting. Allow students time to paste their words on a piece of paper. Check to see if students put them into the correct order. Students could then illustrate each of these words.

14. Read Fleming's *In the Small, Small Pond* to students. Ask students, "Can you think of a place where animals live that you could see the seasons change?" Have the class select one habitat. Some ideas might include the forest, the farm, or the prairie. Have students generate a list of animals that live in the habitat and write these animals on the board. Have each student pick an animal. The teacher should also choose an animal. Using construction paper, show students how to tear paper to create an animal, such as a pig. Simply select a pink piece of construction paper. Tear a circular shape for a head and a large rounded oval for a body. Tear four short fat strips for legs, a squiggly shape for a tail, and two small triangular-shaped ears. Next, glue the pieces together to form a pig. Glue the pig to a piece of heavy white paper. Explain to students that you have decided to show your animal in the hot summer months. Next, tear out a sun and green grass and glue these pieces on your paper. Color your summer sky blue. Add the caption "A pig plays in the sun." Tell students this demonstration shows how a page can be developed for their classroom

book. Have students create their pages in a similar fashion. Explain to students that the pages of the book should show all the seasons and will be put together to create a book on seasons. The teacher may have to write the students' captions on their papers. Bind the finished book and display in the classroom. Students will enjoy reading their own work over and over.

15. Read Calmenson's *Hotter Than a Hot Dog!* to students. This book is best read on a warm August or May day. Ask students the following questions and record their responses on the chalkboard:

   - What reminds you of the heat of the summer?
   - What do you wear in the heat of the summer?
   - What do you do to cool off?
   - What foods do you like to eat in the summer?

Make ice pops with students using fruit juice and ice cube trays. Allow students to eat their ice pops on the school playground.

16. Prior to this activity, the teacher should write the following words on several index cards: windy, calm, breezy, and gusty. Discuss and define each of these terms by taking the class outside each day to determine the degree of windiness for two weeks. Read Carlstrom's *How Does the Wind Walk?* to the students. Explain to students that for two weeks the class will keep a wind chart. Tell students that they will determine the degree of windiness each day. The teacher should put the corresponding index card on the calendar to indicate the students' findings.

17. Before sharing Maass' *When Spring Comes*, have students discuss what changes spring brings in their community. List their ideas on the chalkboard. Some of their ideas might include: plants turn green, snow melts, and flowers bloom. After sharing the book, add to the list on the chalkboard. Have students draw a picture of their favorite part of spring. Allow them to dictate a sentence to the teacher or a parent telling about their picture. Compile all the pictures to make a class book. Share the book with students. Use Maass' *When Summer Comes* to do a similar activity.

18. Before sharing Hest's *Ruby's Storm*, instruct students to listen for words describing the spring storm that Ruby walked through. Read the story and ask students to tell what words described the storm. Write their words on the chalkboard. Then provide students with a piece of white 8½" x 11" paper and crayons. Tell students that, on this sheet of paper, they need to draw a picture depicting one action that the storm displayed. For example, they may want to draw a picture of the storm turning people's umbrellas inside out or newspapers flying in the wind. Then allow time for students to share their drawings with the class.

19. Read Patron's *Dark Cloud Strong Breeze* to students. After sharing, have the students act out the story using sounds in the book. There are sounds that go with the door, dog, locksmith, grocer, cat, butterfly, rain, mice, boxes, and keys. Have students select actions to go with each sound. The remainder of the students could be the rain. Ask students if they have ever been caught in a storm. Where were they? What did they do? Were they frightened? Allow time for students to discuss their answers.

20. Prior to sharing Hirschi's two books, *Spring* and *Winter*, ask students to listen for the different kinds of animals Hirschi mentions. Read both books to students. After the books are read, write the words "Winter" and "Spring" on the chalkboard. Under the Winter column, ask students to list the names of animals mentioned in the book. Do the same for Spring. Have students determine if any animals were common to both books. Make a list of these animals and then reread the books. This time, ask students to look and listen to determine the differences in the habitats of these animals. Discuss these differences. Next, have students think of their own pets and ask how they are different in the winter and in the spring.

■

SPACE

STUDENT OBJECTIVES

1. Recognize that the sun gives us heat and light.
2. Identify the earth as one of the nine planets in our solar system.
3. Identify the fact that the earth has one moon.
4. Identify elements of the solar system, including planets, moon, and sun.

RECOMMENDED READINGS

Babcock, Chris. *No Moon, No Milk!* Illustrated by Mark Teague. Crown, 1993. (Objective 3)
Martha the cow refuses to give milk until she gets to go to the moon.

Branley, Franklyn M. *The Planets in Our Solar System.* Illustrated by Don Madden. Crowell, 1987. (Objective 2)
This factual book provides information about the planets.

————. *The Sun: Our Nearest Star*. Illustrated by Don Madden. HarperCollins, 1988. (Objective 1)
This information book explains the importance of the sun for the everyday existence of human beings.

Bulla, Clyde Robert. *What Makes a Shadow?* Illustrated by June Otani. HarperCollins, 1994. (Objective 1)
This simple information book offers descriptions, explanations, and activities about shadows.

Carle, Eric. *Papa, Please Get the Moon for Me*. Picture Book Studio, 1986. (Objectives 3 & 4)
A little girl asks her father to bring the moon home for her as a playmate.

Coffelt, Nancy. *Dogs in Space*. Harcourt Brace Jovanovich, 1993. (Objective 2)
Through dogs, students learn basic information about each of the nine planets.

Farber, Norma. *Return of the Shadows*. Illustrated by Andrea Baruffi. HarperCollins, 1992. (Objective 1)
Mixed-up shadows are displayed in this playful book.

Field, Susan. *The Sun, the Moon, and the Silver Baboon*. HarperCollins, 1993. (Objectives 1 & 3)
Field's story explains how the sun and the moon were instrumental in providing the baboon with his colorful coat.

Gollub, Matthew. *The Moon Was at a Fiesta*. Illustrated by Leovigildo Martinez. Tambourine Books, 1994. (Objectives 1, 3, & 4)
The moon gets discouraged after seeing what fun the sun gets to have every day.

Ichikawa, Satomi. *Nora's Stars*. Philomel, 1989. (Objective 4)
Nora takes the stars for her own playthings but decides she doesn't like the dark and sad night.

London, Jonathan. *Into the Night We Are Rising*. Illustrated by G. Brian Karas. Viking, 1993. (Objectives 3 & 4)
Children are shown flying above the earth as they dream.

Miranda, Anne. *Night Songs*. Bradbury Press, 1993. (Objectives 3 & 4)
Collage illustrations beautifully depict the night sky and the noisemakers that come out in the dark.

Murphy, Bryan. *Experiment with Light*. Lerner, 1991. (Objective 1)
Murphy outlines simple principles of light.

Paul, Ann Whitford. *Shadows Are About.* Illustrated by Mark Graham. Scholastic, 1992. (Objective 1)
Beautiful poetry and illustrations show shadows in a variety of places.

Yolen, Jane. *What Rhymes with Moon?* Illustrated by Ruth Tietjer Councell. Philomel, 1993. (Objectives 1 & 4)
Yolen writes a beautiful collection of poems about the moon.

GROUP INTRODUCTORY ACTIVITY

Preparing for the Activity: Locate Branley's *The Planets in Our Solar System* and print the following words on 3" x 5" index cards (one word per card): sun, asteroids, comets, meteoroids, Mercury, Venus, Earth, Mars, Jupiter, Saturn, Uranus, Neptune, and Pluto. Make enough cards so that each student has one. Have available a long wall space or bulletin board.

Focus: Before reading Branley's book, have each student choose a card from a basket. Tell students they will need to listen for specific information about the word listed on their card. Be sure to read students the word on their card. Read Branley's book to students. After reading, write the word from each student's card on the board. Ask students to tell one fact they remember from the reading. The teacher should record the students' responses on the board.

Objective: To satisfy the objectives of identifying the Earth as one of the nine planets, recognizing that the Earth has one moon, and identifying the elements of the solar system, students will create a solar system model on the wall. This activity is explained on pages 30 and 31 of the book. After students have put the planets in their correct places, have them tell something they learned about their planet from Branley's book. Students who choose the words asteroids, sun, comets, and meteoroids should make replicas of their objects and place them in the mural.

Extending Activity: Provide time for students to share their wall mural with different classes. Make sure each student has an opportunity to share information on her or his addition to the wall mural.

FOLLOW-UP ACTIVITIES FOR
TEACHER AND STUDENTS TO SHARE

1. Before reading Coffelt's *Dogs in Space,* have a simple poster of the planets prepared and displayed in the classroom. While reading the story, point to each of the planets. Have students draw one planet name out of a hat. Act as the narrator and read the text as students act out the book for the planet they selected. They may need to bring some props from home; for example, Mercury needs sunglasses, Jupiter needs kites, and Neptune needs sweaters. Have students come up with ideas for asteroids and Saturn's 18

moons. After students have practiced, have them present their play to parents or other classes.

2. Before reading Ichikawa's *Nora's Stars*, cut out stars from cardboard and have the students cover their stars with foil. Read the story and then have the students act out Nora's story.

3. Before reading Field's *The Sun, the Moon, and the Silver Baboon*, tell students to listen carefully to the jobs of the sun and the moon. After sharing the story, write "The Sun" on one side of the chalkboard and "The Moon" on the other side of the chalkboard. Have students explain what each did during the story. Write their ideas on the chalkboard. Then have students discuss what might happen if the sun and the moon both appeared in the sky at the same time.

4. Gather two small paper cups, soil, and four bean seeds per student for this activity. Share Branley's *The Sun: Our Nearest Star* with students. Have students perform the experiment on pages 20 through 25 of the book. After completing the experiment, each student should make a simple bar graph depicting the results. This activity would be a good follow-up to Field's *The Sun, the Moon, and the Silver Baboon*.

5. Before reading Miranda's *Night Songs*, ask students to look at the book's illustrations and find common items among them. Students should mention the moon, stars, and night sky. After the reading, give students the following materials: an assortment of white and yellow fabric; an 11" x 17" sheet of paper; yellow, white, silver, and gold crayons; black watercolor or diluted black tempera paint; and paintbrushes. Have students draw the moon and stars on their paper with the crayons and then have them paint the background of their paper with the black paint. Allow the paper to dry. Have students cut moon shapes from the fabric and glue the shapes to their pictures. Display students' work in the school.

6. After reading London's *Into the Night We Are Rising*, ask students, "What did you see in the sky? What did the sun bring?" Cover one wall in your classroom with white paper. Supply students with a variety of materials, including tempera paint, crayons, scraps of wrapping paper, and scraps of fabric. Ask students to create a mural that starts with children in bed and follows the book through children flying in the night sky to the sunlight. It will be helpful to divide students into small groups and assign each group to a specific part of the mural. Allow several class periods for completion of this activity. When students have finished the mural, invite them to describe the completed project to other classes.

7. Read Farber's *Return of the Shadows* and discuss with the class the possibility of mixing up shadows. Take students outside to look at their own shadows and those of buildings, plants, and equipment on the school grounds. Now share Paul's *Shadows Are About* with students. Darken your

classroom. Using the light from a large flashlight or from an overhead projector, invite students to come forward and make shadow designs on the wall using their hands.

8. Read the following sections of Murphy's *Experiment with Light* to the class: "What Is the Light?" and "Sundials and Eclipses." The sundial activity on pages 6 and 7 can be easily implemented in your classroom. The silhouette activity on page 7 can be done by pairs of students. After completing both activities, discuss where light comes from and why it is important.

9. Before sharing Gollub's *The Moon Was at a Fiesta*, divide students into two groups. One group will represent the sun and the other group will represent the moon. Provide the sun group with a giant cut out of the sun and the moon group with a giant cut out of the moon. Have an adult helper or an older student available to help each group. Then instruct the sun group to list all the things the sun supervises or sees everyday. Instruct the moon group to list what the moon sees every night. After students have compiled their lists, bring the students back together into one big group. Have each group share its list. Then ask students which they would rather be—the sun or the moon? Which sees more? Which has more fun? Now read Gollub's book to the students and then discuss what the sun and the moon got to see in this story.

10. Over several days, share Yolen's *What Rhymes with Moon?* with students. Upon completion of the book, divide students into two groups. One group will be the sun and the other group will be the stars. Have available for students a variety of poetry books from the library. Make sure the books include poems about the sun and the stars. Allow students to work with a partner within their group. This activity requires that some parent volunteers or older students be available. Have each pair of students decide on their favorite poem about the sun or stars. When students have chosen their favorite poem, have them work together to make an illustration to go with their poem. Then have students recite their poem to the class.

11. This activity will require students to be outside. Read Bulla's *What Makes a Shadow?* to students. Divide the class into two groups. Give each student in one group a paper towel; give each student in the other group a book. (Students may use any book in their desk for this activity.) Pair each member of one group with a member of the other group. Follow the directions on pages 18 and 19 to show students what makes some shadows darker than others. Each member of a pair should show her or his partner the results of the pair's experiment. Now return to the classroom and demonstrate the experiment on pages 24 through 26 to show students how to make large and small shadows. Next, using an overhead

projector and a darkened room, demonstrate several of the shadow figures on pages 28 and 29 to students. Give each student the opportunity to make her or his own shadow figures for the rest of the class.

12. Read Babcock's *No Moon, No Milk!* to students and then return to the page that shows the cow on the moon with the American flag. Ask the students if they've ever seen a photograph showing the American flag on the moon. Discuss with students the first landing on the moon. Provide pictures and a video of the first moon landing for students to view.

13. Share Carle's *Papa, Please Get the Moon for Me* with students. Tell students that they will be making a mural that shows the moon in its different phases or sizes. Put a huge piece of white kraft paper on one wall of the classroom. Have students use large brushes and a variety of shades of blue tempera paint to paint the background of the mural. Allow this to dry overnight. Next, divide your class into two groups. One group will make the stars and the other group will make the moon in its various phases. Provide the star group with gold tempera paint and stencils of stars to trace and cut out. Provide the moon group with silver tempera paint and stencils of the moon's phases to cut out. As students complete a star or a phase of the moon, have them add their creations to the mural. Invite other classes to visit the moon mural.

■

ENERGY AND MOTION

STUDENT OBJECTIVES

1. Identify the forces of lifting, pushing, and pulling.
2. Identify simple machines that make work and life easier.
3. Identify different kinds of energy.

RECOMMENDED READINGS

Crews, Donald. *Light.* Greenwillow, 1981. (Objective 3)
   Crews provides readers with a variety of light sources.

Gibbons, Gail. *How a House Is Built.* Holiday House, 1990. (Objectives 1 & 2)
   Gibbons provides a detailed explanation of a house being built.

————. *New Road!* Thomas Y. Crowell, 1983. (Objectives 1 & 2)
Gibbons explains all the important aspects of how a new road is built.

————. *Tool Book.* Holiday House, 1982. (Objectives 1 & 2)
Gibbons classifies a variety of tools in this picture book.

————. *Up Goes the Skyscraper!* Macmillan, 1986. (Objectives 1 & 2)
Gibbons provides a lot of information about building a skyscraper.

Howland, Naomi. *ABCDrive! A Car Trip Alphabet.* Clarion, 1994. (Objective 2)
A delightful ABC book that depicts things that go.

Kelley, True. *Hammers and Mops, Pencils and Pots: A First Book of Tools and Gadgets We Use Around the House.* Crown, 1994. (Objective 2)
This picture book identifies common household tools and simple machines.

Rockwell, Anne. *Things That Go.* E. P. Dutton, 1986. (Objectives 1 & 2)
Rockwell provides simple illustrations and names of things that go in 10 different categories.

Royston, Angela. *Big Machines.* Illustrated by Terry Pastor. Little, Brown and Company, 1994. (Objective 2)
Royston briefly describes a variety of large machines.

Schertle, Alice. *In My Treehouse.* Illustrations by Meredith Dunham. Lothrop, Lee & Shepard, 1983. (Objectives 1 & 2)
A young girl enjoys spending time in her treehouse.

GROUP INTRODUCTORY ACTIVITY

Preparing for the Activity: Locate a copy of Rockwell's *Things That Go* and explain to students that each day they will be discussing things that go. Have old magazines, scissors, and glue available for students to use.

Focus: Rockwell's *Things That Go* encompasses 10 different areas. Each day the teacher and class will discuss one of the areas. For the first day's activities, instruct students to use the materials provided for them to find a picture of something that goes "on the road." Prepare a large "road" on a table top or on the floor of the classroom. Make the road out of black kraft paper and paint yellow strips down the center. Allow time for students to find and cut out a picture. As students cut out their pictures, have them place their pictures on the road. Take time to look over additions with the class. Then share the "On the Road" pages of Rockwell's book. Ask students, "How is a tow truck helpful? How many places do we go in a car every day? What other vehicles are important to us?" Do similar activities for each section of Rockwell's book.

Objective: To help students identify the forces of lifting, pushing, and pulling and the simple machines that make work and life easier, do activities similar to the one above for each section of Rockwell's book. After each section, ask students questions that make them think of the jobs and purpose of the different machines.

Extending Activity: For the different sections of Rockwell's book, provide students with an area to place their findings for that day. Also provide a variety of ways for students to compile objects for that day's lesson. For example, the day before sharing the section in Rockwell's book entitled "Things In the Air," ask students to bring something from home that goes in the air. When students come to class the next day, have a big piece of blue kraft paper, representing the sky, across the chalkboard for students to attach their item.

FOLLOW-UP ACTIVITIES FOR
TEACHER AND STUDENTS TO SHARE

1. Before reading Gibbons' *Up Goes The Skyscraper!*, ask students to listen carefully for information about all the different kinds of machines used to help build a skyscraper. Share Gibbons' book with students and then allow students to make a list of all the different kinds of machines used in the book. Have students work in groups to decide the function of each machine and why that machine was needed to build a skyscraper. Next, provide students with a variety of materials to build a replica of their favorite machine—cereal boxes, toilet paper rolls, string, construction paper, and any other "building type" materials. Students could begin collecting these materials and bringing them from home. Have each group construct their favorite machine and explain how it is used.

2. The day before sharing Crews' *Light*, tell students to go home and look at all the different ways light is used in and around their homes. The next day, make a list of the students' observations on a huge cut out of a light bulb. Choose one item on the list to cover with a small piece of paper so that the item is no longer visible. Then have students discuss how different life would be without that item. Ask students to think about what changes they would need to make in their life if that particular light source were no longer available. Do this same activity with a variety of the items on the list. Then share Crews' *Light* with students and add Crews' ideas to the giant light bulb.

3. Before sharing Gibbons' *New Road!*, tell students to listen carefully for all the different kinds of machines that are needed to build a new road. Then share Gibbons' book with the class. After sharing, take a moment to list the machines mentioned in the story. Provide each student with an 8½" x 11" sheet of white paper, crayons, and pencils. Have students draw a

picture of their favorite machine from Gibbons' book and then explain what their machine is used for. Have a parent volunteer or older student help write the students' words on the bottom of their papers. Compile students pictures into a book, bind the book, and it share with class.

4. Before sharing Gibbons' *Tool Book*, prepare and mount a large variety of tool pictures on pieces of white posterboard and laminate the posters. Ask students which tools they can name. Then ask students to tell what each tool does. Include the following tools: hammer, shovel, tape measure, screwdriver, wrench, drill, ax, hand saw, mallet, pliers, pry bar, brick trowel, and putty knife. Ask for volunteers to take home any pictures that could not be identified. Ask students to ask their mom or dad for help in naming them and identifying how they are used. Allow time for students to share their information the next day with the rest of the class. Share Gibbons' book with students. Next, take the laminated pictures and have students classify them into areas used in Gibbons' book: Tools that measure, Tools that cut, Tools that grip, Tools that make holes, Tools that lift and move things, and Tools that cover surfaces. It would also be fun to have a woodworking area in the classroom for students to practice using some of the tools mentioned in the book.

5. Before sharing Schertle's *In My Treehouse*, have students participate in a roleplaying activity. Give each student some personal space and explain to them that they are now in their very own treehouse. Discuss with students what they would like to do in their treehouse. Some might choose to play, read, or eat, among other things. Explain to students that they will need to use their imaginations for the next part of this activity, then describe the following scene to the students:

> The phone just rang and it's your best friend wanting to come play. How will you get the message? How will your friend get into your treehouse?

List all student suggestions on the board before reading Schertle's story to students. Have them compare her ideas with their ideas. Try out the bucket system used in the story by stringing up a bucket on a playground tree and raising and lowering a variety of objects in the bucket.

6. Before sharing Gibbons' *How a House Is Built*, have students talk about their homes. Discuss with students what kind of homes they live in and ask the following questions:

- Do you live in an apartment or a house?
- What materials were used to build your home?

While sharing Gibbons' book, have students listen for all the different people that work on a house. Make a list of these people after the story is read and add to the list the kinds of tools each of them used. Invite a variety of these people from the community into the classroom to share briefly what they do and what tools they use.

7. After sharing Howland's *ABCDrive! A Car Trip Alphabet*, ask students to name other modes of transportation that travel in water, by air, in space, or by rail. List the students' responses on the chalkboard. Next, ask each student to select one vehicle from the list. Have them illustrate that vehicle and label it. Bind all the vehicle pages to form a transportation book to be shared with the class and then displayed in the library.

8. Before reading Kelley's *Hammers and Mops, Pencils and Pots: A First Book of Tools and Gadgets We Use Around the House* to students, divide the class into groups using the following page headings from Kelley's book: Time to Clean, In the Office, In the Kitchen, Out in the Garden, In the Workshop, and In the Art Room. Allow each group to make a list of all the tools, gadgets, and simple machines that they might find in their area. Now read Kelley's book and compare their responses with those in the book. Students may wish to bring a sample of the items they named from home to share with classmates.

9. Share Royston's *Big Machines* and then discuss the actions of each machine. For example:

garbage truck—squashes

snowblower—churns

combine—shakes

Then take a walk through the neighborhood, telling students to watch for any kind of machine they see working. Upon returning to the classroom, make a list of all the machines students saw on their walk. Then have students think of one word that describes the work that each machine does.

■

ECOLOGY

STUDENT OBJECTIVES

1. Develop an awareness of the concept of "life cycle."
2. Identify commonly used natural resources and ways to conserve them.
3. Develop an understanding of plant and animal habitats.

RECOMMENDED READINGS

Amsel, Sheri. *A Wetland Walk*. Millbrook Press, 1993. (Objective 3)
Beautiful pictures and simple text depict life in the wetlands.

The Big Book for Our Planet. Written by Aliki, et al. Illustrated by Aliki, et al. Dutton Children's Books, 1993. (Objectives 2 & 4)
This selection of beautiful and moving short stories, illustrations, and poems focuses on our planet, Earth.

Brown, Laurie Krasny, and Brown, Marc. *Dinosaurs to the Rescue!* Little, Brown and Company, 1992. (Objective 2)
Clever illustrations coupled with witty text outline ways dinosaurs and humans can help the environment.

Gackenbach, Dick. *The Mighty Tree*. Harcourt Brace Jovanovich, 1992. (Objective 2)
This story follows the lives of three trees from seed to adulthood.

Geraghty, Paul. *Stop That Noise!* Crown, 1992. (Objective 2)
Story of rain forest animals who are awakened by the sounds of a machine destroying their homes.

Greene, Carol. *The Old Ladies Who Liked Cats*. Photographs by Loretta Krupinski. HarperCollins 1991. (Objective 1)
Greene gives very simple explanations of how living things depend on one another for survival.

Guiberson, Brenda Z. *Cactus Hotel*. Illustrated by Megan Lloyd. Henry Holt and Company, 1991. (Objectives 1 & 3)
A saguaro cactus plays host to a variety of animals throughout its lifetime.

Rauzon, Mark J., and Bix, Cynthia Overbeck. *Water, Water Everywhere*. Sierra Club Books for Children, 1994. (Objective 2)
Beautiful photographs show the many uses, properties, and problems of water in our world.

Showers, Paul. *Where Does the Garbage Go?* Illustrated by Randy Chewning. HarperCollins, 1994. (Objective 1)
This book explains landfills, recycling, and the importance of both.

GROUP INTRODUCTORY ACTIVITY

Preparing for the Activity: Locate a copy of Geraghty's *Stop That Noise!* and have materials ready for students to create costumes or puppets based on the animals in the book. These materials should include fabric scraps, construction paper, tongue depressors, popsicle sticks, glue, sequins, and any other available collage materials.

Focus: Tell students that they will be listening to a story about a place in which the animals are in danger. Tell them to listen and watch carefully to find out where the story takes place, what animals are involved, and what is causing them to be in danger. Share Geraghty's book.

Objective: To satisfy the objective of understanding ways to conserve natural resources, students should discuss what will happen to the animals in this habitat if all the trees are cut down. Take a walk around the school and playground. Ask students to think about what habitats are in the area. Ask students if they see anything that might be disruptive to these habitats. Their answers might include building taking place nearby, or even students playing on the playground and disrupting the ants' habitat.

Extending Activity: Reread Geraghty's book, this time allowing students to make the animal and machine noises in the book. Animals in the book include a tree mouse, frogs, hummingbirds, toucans, a macaw, monkeys, and cats. Let each student choose an animal he or she would like to act out. Provide materials from which students can make stick puppets. Read the story a third time, allowing students to hold up their puppets and make the appropriate noises. Invite another class in to see the production.

FOLLOW-UP ACTIVITIES FOR
TEACHER AND STUDENTS TO SHARE

1. Read the Browns' *Dinosaurs to the Rescue!* to students. Ask each student to select one environmental tip to illustrate. Explain to students that each page will be part of a classroom book. The teacher can label each page with the tip the student chose to illustrate. Have a Create-A-Cover Contest. Ask students to submit designs for the cover of the classroom book. After students have submitted their covers, display them in the class for one week. Then have the class select their favorite cover.

2. Before sharing Gackenbach's *The Mighty Tree*, make two big trees out of kraft paper. On one tree, write "What It Can Be," and on the other tree, write "What It Is." Then divide the class into two groups. Make sure each group has a parent volunteer or older student who is able to record student responses. Allow each group five to ten minutes to brainstorm ideas to list on their tree. It would be appropriate to provide students with a few examples before they begin. Then have students switch groups. Allow these new groups another five to ten minutes to add their ideas to the tree. Read Gackenbach's book to students and then have them review the lists that they made and add to them if necessary.

3. Before sharing Greene's *The Old Ladies Who Liked Cats*, divide the class into pairs and have each pair of students prepare simple pictures of the following: sailors, milk/cows, clover, bees, mice, and cats. Each pair of students should have a set of the pictures. Then share the story with students. After sharing provide each pair of students with paper, glue, and crayons. Instruct students to paste their pictures in a circular design on their paper; this design should show the relationship each picture has to one another. For example, the sailor and the cow would be next to each other because the cow's milk provides the sailor with a nutritious food. Students should draw arrows between the pictures to show the dependence of each person or animal on the other.

4. Before sharing Rauzon and Bix's *Water, Water Everywhere*, make a huge cut out of a water faucet with a big water drop coming out of the faucet. Ask students to help list all the ways that they use water every day on this huge cut out. After sharing the book, have students discuss ways that they can conserve water. Arrange a field trip to a local water treatment plant. Upon returning from the field trip, have students discuss what they learned on the field trip and add to the list on the cut out.

5. Share Guiberson's *Cactus Hotel* with students. Have cut outs of the following stages of the saguaro cactus' life ready for students upon finishing the story: black seeds, a young cactus, a 25-year-old cactus, a 50-year-old cactus, a 60-year-old cactus, a 150-year-old cactus, and a 200-year-old cactus. Divide students into groups to work on each stage of the cactus' life. Provide materials for students to make drawings of the animals that lived in, on, or around the cactus during each time period. Display the various stages around the room and invite classes in to tell them about each stage of the saguaro cactus.

6. Before reading Amsel's *A Wetland Walk*, ask students the following questions:

   • Have you ever been to a wetland area, like a swamp or bog?
   • What did the area look like?
   • What plants did you see?
   • What animals did you see?
   • If you have not been to a wetland area, what animals and plants do you think you might see?
   • Where do you think you might find wetland areas?
   • Are there any wetlands close to our school or your neighborhood?

   Record the students' responses on the board. Read Amsel's *A Wetland Walk* to students and ask them to listen for answers to the questions that they answered previously. Compare their experiences with wetlands to those described in the book. If possible, visit a wetland area near the school.

7. Before sharing Showers' *Where Does the Garbage Go?*, prepare a bulletin board in the classroom similar to the one in the story: "What Are We Doing to Help the Environment?" Then ask students for their ideas on what they are doing to help the environment. Next, share the story with students. Contact a local landfill or recycling center and take a field trip there if possible. The book shows the recycling sign. Ask students to go home and look for this symbol on products in their home. Ask them to bring an example to school. After sharing the book, have students add ideas to the class bulletin board. Then have the class select one idea in which they would like to see the entire school participate.

8. Read Hoban's "Take Time" from *The Big Book for Our Planet* to students. After reading, take students for a walk around the neighborhood. Remind students of the words Hoban used, remembering to stop and look "closely and carefully" at things they find interesting. Upon returning to class, provide each student with an 8½" x 11" sheet of white construction paper and crayons. Instruct students to draw and color the one thing they found most interesting, intriguing, and wondrous during their walk. Allow time for students to share their drawings with classmates.

9. Share McPhail's "Pigs on Patrol" from *The Big Book for Our Planet* with students. Practice the last verse with students. Recite this verse each day while participating in the following activity. Before beginning this activity, explain to students that they will be removing paper and aluminum cans from the playground. Further explain that other items, such as glass, clothing, plastic, and metal will need to be picked up by the school custodian. The teacher will want to have the help of several adult volunteers for this activity. Tell students that each week they will pick up trash from the school playground. Each student should be asked to bring some paper garbage sacks to school. Choose one day a week for students to spend the last 15 minutes of school collecting trash from the playground. Put the trash they collect into the paper garbage sacks and keep a weekly chart depicting how many paper sacks full of trash they collect. Do this project for a nine-week period. Add to the chart each week. After the nine-week period, ask students to refer to the chart to answer the following questions:

   • Which week did they pick up the least amount of trash?
   • Which week did they pick up the most trash?
   • How many sacks of trash did they gather altogether?

   Display the chart in the hall for other classes to see.

■

NONPRINT SOURCES FOR K-T-1

Prior to using any of these nonprint sources, read all of the accompanying documentation and preview the application. The literature accompanying many of these products suggests appropriate uses. Determine if the material is to be used by the entire class, by small groups of students, or by an individual student. After choosing the audience for the nonprint material selected, it will be necessary to teach students how to use the application.

LIFE SCIENCE—ANIMALS

The Treehouse. Broderbund Software, Inc., 1991. Mac or MS-DOS software.
  This multi-disciplinary program allows students to learn about over 90 animals.

A World of Animals. National Geographic Society, 1993. Mac CD-ROM.
  This computer book provides students with an interactive approach to learning and recalling information about animals.

LIFE SCIENCE—PLANTS

Woolly's Garden. MECC. Apple II software.
  This simulation allows students to explore plant growth.

A World of Plants. National Geographic Society, 1993. Mac CD-ROM.
  This computer book provides students with an interactive approach to learning and recalling information about plants.

HUMAN BODY

The Human Body. National Geographic Society, 1993. Mac CD-ROM.
  This computer book provides students with an interactive approach to learning and recalling information about the human body.

EARTH SCIENCE

Our Earth. National Geographic Society, 1993. Mac CD-ROM.
  This computer book provides students with an interactive approach to learning and recalling information about the Earth.

ENERGY AND MOTION

Woolly Bounce. MECC, 1991. Apple II software.
This simulation allows students to explore bouncing balls.

ECOLOGY

Eco-Saurus. Davidson & Associates, Inc., 1991. MS-DOS software.
This ecology awareness program introduces young students to basic ecology and conservation concepts.

CHAPTER

Second Grade/Third Grade

■

LIFE SCIENCE—ANIMALS

STUDENT OBJECTIVES

1. Classify animals according to the habitats in which they live.
2. Know the proper care of animals.
3. Be aware of animal survival techniques such as color change, hibernation, and migration.

RECOMMENDED READINGS

Alexander, Sally Hobart. *Maggie's Whopper*. Illustrated by Deborah Kogan Ray. MacMillan, 1992. (Objective 3)
Alexander tells a heart warming story of an uncle and niece who both love to fish and their encounter with Thatch, the bear.

Arnosky, Jim. *Every Autumn Comes the Bear*. G.P. Putnam's Sons, 1993. (Objective 3)
The bear comes to the farm in autumn to prepare for his winter hibernation.

———. *A Kettle of Hawks and Other Wildlife Groups*. Lothrop, Lee & Shepard, 1990. (Objective 3)
Each page tells the name for a group of a specific animal and gives a variety of information about the animal.

Auch, Mary Jane. *Bird Dogs Can't Fly*. Holiday House, 1993. (Objectives 1, 2, & 3)
This is a delightful story of a dog who befriends a goose during hunting season.

Bash, Barbara. *Shadows of the Night: The Hidden World of the Little Brown Bat.* Sierra Club Books for Children, 1993. (Objectives 1 & 3)
A delightful information book about the only flying mammal.

Bernhard, Emery, and Bernhard, Durga. *Eagles: Lions of the Sky.* Holiday House, 1994. (Objectives 1, 2, & 3)
This information book describes the eagle, its hunting practices, its history, its habitat, and its symbolism.

Blake, Robert J. *The Perfect Spot.* Philomel Books, 1992. (Objective 1)
A painter and his son walk through the woods searching for "the perfect spot."

Charles, Donald. *Ugly Bug.* Dial, 1994. (Objectives 1 & 3)
One bug is considered particularly ugly until he meets one of his own.

Florian, Douglas. *Beast Feast.* Harcourt Brace & Company, 1994. (Objectives 1, 2, & 3)
Fun watercolor paintings and poems illustrate a wide variety of animals.

Gibbons, Gail. *Frogs.* Holiday House, 1993 (Objectives 1 & 3)
This information book describes the transformation from egg to frog.

———. *Monarch Butterfly.* Holiday House, 1989. (Objective 2)
Gibbons follows the monarch butterfly through its life cycle.

———. *Sharks.* Holiday House, 1992. (Objectives 1 & 3)
Gibbons describes sharks, their behavior, habitat, and survival.

———. *Spiders.* Holiday House, 1993. (Objectives 1 & 3)
This information book describes spiders, their habits and habitats.

Gove, Doris. *One Rainy Night.* Illustrated by Walter Lyon Krudop. Atheneum, 1994. (Objective 1)
A family catches and releases a variety of animals for a nature center.

Hendrick, Mary Jean. *If Anything Ever Goes Wrong At the Zoo....* Illustrated by Jane Dyer. Harcourt Brace Jovanovich, 1993. (Objective 2)
Leslie finds out what happens when she tells the zookeeper that if anything goes wrong at the zoo the animals can come to her house.

Hirschi, Ron. *A Time for Babies.* Photographs by Thomas D. Mangelsen. Cobblehill Books, 1993. (Objective 1)
Descriptive photographs and text beautifully illustrate animal parents caring for their young.

———. *Who Lives in...the Forest?* Photographs by Galen Burrell. Dodd, Mead & Company, 1987. (Objective 1)
Simple text and beautiful photographs introduce the animals of the forest.

————. *Who Lives in...the Mountains?* Photographs by Galen Burrell. G.P. Putnam's Sons, 1989. (Objective 1)
Simple text and beautiful photographs introduce the animals of the mountains.

————. *Who Lives on...the Prairie?* Photographs by Galen Burrell. G.P Putnam's Sons, 1989. (Objective 1)
Simple text and beautiful photographs introduce the animals of the prairie.

Irvine, Joan. *Build It with Boxes.* Illustrated by Linda Hendry. Morrow Junior Books, 1993. (Objective 1)
Irvine provides many fun projects to make with boxes.

James, Simon. *Dear Mr. Blueberry.* Macmillan, 1991. (Objectives 1, 2, & 3)
The reader learns about whales from letters written back and forth between a girl and her teacher.

Keller, Holly. *Island Baby.* Greenwillow, 1992. (Objective 2)
Pops and Simon take care of a variety of island birds, including one special flamingo.

Lauber, Patricia. *Snakes Are Hunters.* Illustrated by Holly Keller. HarperCollins, 1988. (Objectives 1 & 3)
Lauber describes how the physical characteristics of snakes make them able hunters.

Lavies, Bianca. *It's an Armadillo!* E. P. Dutton, 1989. (Objective 3)
Photographs and text provide insights into the unusual world of the armadillo.

Machotka, Hana. *Outstanding Outsides.* Morrow Junior Books, 1993. (Objective 3)
Machotka describes the many different functions of animal outsides.

Markle, Sandra. *Outside and Inside Spiders.* Macmillan, 1994. (Objectives 1, 2, & 3)
Graphic photographs illustrate the spider's life cycle, habitat, mating habits, and physical appearance.

Martin, Jacqueline Briggs. *Good Times on Grandfather Mountain.* Illustrated by Susan Gaber. Orchard Books, 1992. (Objective 2)
Old Washburn whittles away, unconcerned about the animal mishaps that create havoc on his farm.

Martin, James. *Hiding Out: Camouflage in the Wild.* Photographs by Art Wolfe. Crown, 1993. (Objective 3)
Beautiful photographs depict a variety of animals' abilities to blend into their habitats.

Most, Bernard. *Zoodles*. Harcourt Brace Jovanovich, 1992. (Objectives 1, 2, & 3)
This clever riddle book puts animals together in a very interesting way.

Oram, Hiawyn. *A Creepy Crawly Song Book*. Music by Carl Davis. Illustrated by Satoshi Kitamura. Farrar, Straus and Giroux, 1993. (Objectives 1, 2, & 3)
This wonderful collection of songs about insects and animals paints a vivid picture for every child.

Rauzon, Mark J. *Horns, Antlers, Fangs, and Tusks*. Lothrop, Lee & Shepard, 1993. (Objective 3)
Colorful photographs and text illustrate the importance to animals of horns, antlers, fangs, and tusks for protection.

————. *Skin, Scales, Feathers, and Fur*. Lothrop, Lee & Shepard, 1993. (Objective 3)
Colorful photographs and text illustrate the importance to animals of skin, scales, feathers, and fur for protection.

Ryder, Joanne. *One Small Fish*. Illustrated by Carol Schwartz. Morrow Junior Books, 1993. (Objective 3)
A bored school girl imagines the world of the deep sea.

Sage, James. *Where the Great Bear Watches*. Illustrated by Lisa Flather. Viking, 1993. (Objective 1)
Sage tells the story of a young Inuit boy who is trying to provide for his family and sled dogs.

Vyner, Sue. *Arctic Spring*. Illustrated by Tim Vyner. Viking, 1992. (Objective 3)
Through colorful illustrations and limited text, Vyner takes the animals of the Arctic from winter hibernation to spring.

Wood, Jakki. *Animal Parade*. Macmillan, 1993. (Objectives 1, 2 & 3)
This alphabet book provides common and uncommon animal names for each letter of the alphabet.

Yolen, Jane. *Animal Fare*. Illustrated by Janet Street. Harcourt Brace & Company, 1994. (Objectives 1, 2, & 3)
Yolen plays on animal names to create delightful poems.

Yoshida, Toshi. *Elephant Crossing*. Philomel, 1989. (Objective 3)
Yoshida follows a herd of elephants as they try to move through an invasion of grasshoppers.

————. *Young Lions*. Philomel, 1989. (Objectives 1 & 3)
Young lions explore their habitat while embarking on their first hunt.

GROUP INTRODUCTORY ACTIVITY

Preparing for the Activity: Locate Bernard Most's *Zoodles*. Provide the following materials for each student: a slip of paper with the name of an animal mentioned in the book, poster board for each pair of students, markers, and a variety of construction paper. Tell students that you will be sharing a few riddles with them.

Focus: Explain to students that this is a book of riddles and that the answer to each riddle is a combination of two animals. After reading the first riddle, allow time for each student to guess what the animal answer might be. After you have shared the answer with the group, let the students who have the names of the two animals sit together. When you have finished the entire book, each student should be sitting with a partner.

Objective: To satisfy the objectives of classifying animals according to their habitats, their proper care, and their survival techniques, have each pair of students create a Venn diagram that includes their animals. The Venn diagram needs to include information on each animal and should depict how the habitat, care, and survival techniques of each animal correspond with those of the other animal in the riddle. Some information should overlap. For example:

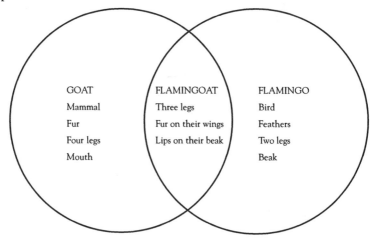

Each group will show and explain their Venn diagram to the entire class.

Extending Activity: Have each pair of students make a clay or playdough model of each of their animals. Then have them work together on a model of their combined animal.

FOLLOW-UP ACTIVITIES FOR
TEACHER AND STUDENTS TO SHARE

1. While reading Alexander's *Maggie's Whopper*, stop periodically and ask students to think about the following questions: Why do you think he stole the pie? What might cause the lack of food? After sharing the story, have students make a short list of things they know about Thatch.

2. After reading Arnosky's *A Kettle of Hawks and Other Wildlife Groups*, have students match the animals mentioned in the book with their group names. Write the names of the animals on the left side of the board and the group names in mixed-up order on the right side of the board. Have different students come up and draw lines to match the animals and group names together. Divide students into seven groups. Have each group choose one of the following animals: clams, whales, chickens, ducks, coyotes, beavers, and wolves. After students find their animals group name, have them make stick puppets, of their animal. To make the stick puppets, provide students with tongue depressors or popsicle sticks, a variety of colors of construction paper, and glue. Then have students present their group name, using their stick puppets, to the entire class.

3. After reading Blake's *The Perfect Spot*, have students list animals mentioned in the story along with characteristics of the habitat in which the animals were found. For example, some habitat characteristics might be wet, dry, rocky, etc. Divide the class into groups to research each animal's habitat and determine if it is correctly depicted in the story. Have the groups report their findings to the entire class.

4. Read Gibbons' *Sharks* and then have students make a book based on an acrostic poem using the word SHARK. To explain acrostic poems, have the class use the word SEA to create a class acrostic poem. Ask students to think of something that lives in the sea beginning with the letter S. Follow the same procedure for "E" and "A". An example would be:

> Shark
>
> Eel
>
> Anemone

Divide the class into groups with five students in each group. Assign some groups to make a book that would use each letter of the word SHARK to describe survival techniques of the shark. For example, for the letter A, students could describe and illustrate the survival mechanisms called "ampullae." Have other groups make an acrostic book describing and illustrating the habitats of different types of sharks. For example, the letter S could stand for "shallow water," where whale sharks and hammerheads swim. After the groups have finished, bind their books and allow time for each group to share their final project with the class.

5. After reading Keller's *Island Baby*, have students make a class list of all the different jobs that Pops and Simon had to do to take care of the birds. Compare that list with the jobs students do to take care of a pet at home or the classroom pet. Students could also try to find out more information on each of the island birds depicted in the book.

6. Before reading Lauber's *Snakes Are Hunters*, tell students that they will become snake specialists. Then share Lauber's book, reminding students to keep in mind a snake they would like to learn more about. As the story is read, point out the snakes' special adaptation mechanisms, such as some snakes' ability to change color to blend into their surroundings. After the story is read, students will select a type of snake mentioned in the book and use the library to research its habitat and special survival adaptations. Have students write their information on a paper snake that they have made to look like their snake.

7. Before reading Martin's *Good Times on Grandfather Mountain*, make a list of the animals mentioned in the story on the chalkboard. Under each animal, list what it would take to care for these animals. Then read the story. Stop in the middle of the story and ask students why they think the animals left. After reading, have students add to their list about caring for animals.

8. Share *Elephant Crossing* with students and discuss how Yoshida follows the herd of elephants through the dangers of their journey. Have students select an endangered species and determine what has endangered it and how it attempts to defend itself. Supply students with 2' by 3' white paper and markers. Ask them to make a poster depicting how humans could help their endangered animal.

9. Divide students into three groups and provide each group with a copy of one of the following Hirschi books: *Who Lives in...the Forest?*, *Who Lives in...the Mountains?*, and *Who Lives on...the Prairie?* Allow enough time for each group to share its book with all group members. Then have each group create its own book, using the following titles:

> Who Lives in...the Ocean?
> Who Lives in...the Desert?
> Who Lives in...the Arctic?

Give students specific information that must be included. For example, they must include 8 to 10 animals, illustrated in their habitat, using one or more of a variety of media, such as collage, watercolor, crayon, or colored pencil. Bind the finished products and have groups share their books with other classrooms.

10. After sharing Gibbons' *Monarch Butterfly*, have students make their own butterfly wings. Gibbons provides a good model in this book. Students will need black construction paper, orange tissue paper, white poster paint, brushes, glue, tape, and black yarn. Wings can be fastened on using yarn looped through the wings and tied on as shown in the book. Allow time for students to parade through the school and share an explanation of the monarch's life cycle with other classrooms.

11. After sharing both Arnosky's *Every Autumn Comes the Bear* and Vyner's *Arctic Spring*, have students list the animals that were in hibernation. Divide students into small groups to research one of the animals they have listed. Use this information to construct a class chart that would include the following information about each of the animals: location, weight, height, distinctive features, food, hibernation habits, and how the animal protects itself from other animals. After students have filled in the chart with the correct information, have them answer the following questions:

    • Which animal hibernates the longest?
    • Which animal is the largest? smallest?
    • Which animal lives the furthest north?
    • Which animals are meat eaters? plant eaters?

12. Before reading the Bernhards' *Eagles: Lions of the Sky*, ask students if they ever noticed a picture of an eagle on anything. Ask each student to go home and find something with an eagle on it that he or she can share with the class. The next day, invite students to share their findings. Ask them to explain why they think an eagle might be a symbol on the items brought from home. Now read the Bernhards' book to the students, and then discuss the qualities of an eagle that make it a good symbol.

13. Share a variety of poems from Florian's *Beast Feast*. Explain to students that they will be creating a class poetry anthology using Florian's book as an example. Poems should be about animals not included in Florian's book and should depict animal characteristics. Titles for the poems should be fashioned after Florian's titles, simply using the name of the animal. Students should then make simple watercolor illustrations of their poems. Paintings and poems can be bound into a classroom book or displayed in a school hall.

14. Ask students what they think of when they hear the word "bat," and then read to them Bash's *Shadows of the Night: The Hidden World of the Little Brown Bat*. List on the board the names of other nocturnal animals suggested by the students. The teacher may have to refer to an encyclopedia for a list of nocturnal animals. Divide students into groups of three or four. Assign each group one nocturnal animal to research. Give each

group a sheet of paper containing the following items, and ask the group members to record their findings on the paper. Groups will need to use library resources to research nocturnal animals.

- Name of the animal:
- Description of the animal:
- Where the animal can be found (what part of the world):
- Where the animal sleeps and when:
- What the animal does at night:
- What features make the animal suited to night life:
- Any other unusual things about the animal:
- A picture of the animal from a magazine or a drawing of the animal:

After research is completed, each group will act as a panel of nocturnal animal specialists. The panel should sit behind a table at the front of the classroom. The panel members will use the information they gathered to answer questions posed by the audience. The audience should be composed of other classes or parents. Have each panel answer 4 or 5 questions.

15. Read Auch's *Bird Dogs Can't Fly* to students. Provide a sheet of 8½" x 11" white paper for each student and instruct the students to fold their papers in half. Next, ask students to write DOG on one side of their paper and GOOSE on the other. Next ask them to list the ways the goose and dog were different in the story. After students have had time to record their answers, discuss them. Important things to include in the discussion would be migration, modes of travel, appearance differences, and habitat differences.

16. Before sharing Sage's *Where the Great Bear Watches*, explain to students that they will use context clues to determine the location of the story. After sharing, show students where the North Pole is on a map. What clues did students use to determine the location of the story? List the animals that were mentioned in the story on the chalkboard. Divide the list into three sections: Animals in the Air, Animals on Land, and Animals in the Sea. Next, provide students with paper to make a huge class mural and divide the class into three groups—water, land, and air. Have construction paper, scissors, markers, and glue available for students to use in constructing replicas of each animal mentioned in the story. Students should then put their animals in the proper place on the mural.

17. Read Hendrick's *If Anything Ever Goes Wrong at the Zoo...*and then ask students to list all the animals that came to Leslie's house. The teacher should print students' responses on the chalkboard. Their list should in-

clude the ostrich, zebra, monkey, lion, elephant, and alligator. Divide students into six groups and give each group one of the animals in Hendrick's book. Using library resources, students should determine what it would take to care for one of these animals and if these things could be done at someone's house. Students will need to answer the following questions during their research:

- What would the animal eat?
- Where would the animal sleep?
- Does the animal need to be kept at a certain temperature?
- Does the animal need to be in water?
- Does the animal require running room?

Students should share their answers with the class.

18. As a fun culminating activity for a unit on animals or insects, select one or two of the songs in Oram's *A Creepy Crawly Song Book* to teach to students. Be sure to share the illustrations for each song selected. Ask the music teacher in your school or a musically inclined parent to assist with this activity; piano or guitar accompaniment would make the songs more exciting for students. After the songs are learned, ask students to create body movements to accompany the lyrics. Each student could be responsible for one line. Have each student teach their movement to the others. Rehearse several times. Students could also create costumes for the insects or animals using construction paper, tissue paper, tape, glue, paint, and yarn. For example, bee wings could be created from black construction paper and yellow tissue paper. These wings could be tied on with yarn, or armholes could actually be made in the construction paper. An antenna headpiece could be made from a strip of two-inch-wide paper fastened to fit each child's head. Strips of black paper could be glued on to form antennae. Students could perform their songs for other classes.

19. After reading Hirschi's *A Time for Babies*, have students name the animals mentioned in the book. List the animal names on the chalkboard and then have students give the appropriate name for each animal baby, e.g., *eagles* and *eaglets*. Discuss what the parents of each baby animal had to provide for the babies to survive. List the students' responses on the chalkboard. Next, ask students to name their pets—dogs, cats, birds, etc.—and write these on the chalkboard. Ask a student to come to the board and write the name of the baby of each of these pets. Have students generate a list of ways people help their pets survive.

20. Share Ryder's *One Small Fish* with students. After reading, have students list some of the sea creatures they saw pictured in this book. Explain to students that animals have certain characteristics that help them to sur-

vive in their habitat. Ask pairs of students to select one of the ocean creatures and research its survival mechanisms. Using the facts about their animal, each pair of students will create an acrostic poem that explains the survival mechanisms and techniques of their animal. An example might be the following acrostic for "eel":

> Electrifying
> Eerie
> Long

21. Show students the title page of Machotka's *Outstanding Outsides* and ask them what kind of animal is pictured. Then have students guess how this animal might protect itself. Proceed through the book, allowing students to speculate on what each animal outside provides that animal. After sharing, allow time for students to discuss the questions on the back page. Next, divide students into small work groups. Each group must come up with an animal to research. They will need to provide a variety of ways their animals' outsides protect them and an illustration of their animal. Provide time for students to share their information and pictures with the class.

22. Trace a picture of an armadillo, perhaps by using the title page of Lavies' *It's an Armadillo!* Enlarge this tracing to make a cut out of an armadillo to give each student before you read this story. Instruct students to listen carefully as you read and to write a fact about each body part of the armadillo on that body part. After reading, ask students to share what they wrote on each body part.

23. Before sharing Wood's *Animal Parade*, provide each student with one letter of the alphabet written on a 3" x 5" index card. Tell students to list animals that begin with their letter on the back of their index card. Give students several minutes to do this activity. Explain to students that while the book is being read they will need to listen for animals on their list. Instruct them to put a mark by each animal that is already on their list, then have them add the names of animals that are not on their list. Share Wood's book; it may be helpful to students to do so several times. After sharing, instruct students to investigate one of the animals mentioned in the book that was not on their list. Have students find five interesting facts and a picture of their animal. Allow several days for this research. Provide time for students to share their information and pictures with the class.

24. Prior to reading Rauzon's *Horns, Antlers, Fangs, and Tusks* and *Skin, Scales, Feathers, and Fur*, ask each student to find a picture of an animal having one of these protective body parts. Ask each student to explain to the class how this body part protects the animal. Read these two books to

students and compare the students' ideas with the facts in the books about animal body parts that are used for protection.

25. Before reading James' *Dear Mr. Blueberry*, give each student a piece of paper and have him or her write the name of an animal on the paper. After reading the story, have students write a letter to another student asking one animal characteristic question. For example, if a student had written "tiger" on the paper, that student's question to another might be: "Dear Mary, Where do tigers live?" Students should trade letters and search for the answer to their question. Have students illustrate their answer and share their information with the class.

FOLLOW-UP ACTIVITIES FOR INDIVIDUALS AND SMALL GROUPS

1. Select three or four other students to work with on this activity. Reread Hendrick's *If Anything Ever Goes Wrong at the Zoo.* . . . Now, create a story similar to Hendrick's book about animals coming to your home from a different location. Animals could be coming from an aquarium, an aviary, or a wilderness park. Give each student working with you on this activity an animal to include in the story. Each member will be responsible for the text and illustration for that animal. Share your finished book with classmates.

2. Select one animal in Martin's *Hiding Out: Camouflage in the Wild* to read about. Carefully study the photograph of that animal in Martin's book. Using construction paper, watercolors, glue, and scissors, create a likeness of the animal you chose. Now make a likeness of this animal's habitat. Paste your animal into its habitat and display it in your classroom.

3. Using the Bernhards' *Eagles: Lions of the Sky* as a model, select a different animal that you might find symbolized on a variety of items. For example, you could look for items that use a bull as part of their logo. Bring a collection of these items from home and display them for classmates.

4. Read Gove's *One Rainy Night* and list the animals mentioned in the story. Think about the environment where these animals were found. Choose one animal and find five facts about that animal. Draw the animal in its habitat and write the five facts on the back of the paper.

5. Read Yoshida's *Young Lions* and use library resources to find out where lions live, how long lions live, and several other unusual facts about lions. Include a map showing where lions live.

6. After the teacher reads several of Yolen's poems from *Animal Fare*, select an animal that Yolen has not included in her book to write about and draw. You will need to think of an object that can be combined with your

animal. After your work is complete, share your poem with your classmates.

7. Read Gibbons' *Frogs* and draw and color a picture of a frog on a white
sheet of paper. Around the frog, draw five lilypads, and on each lilypad
write one unusual fact about frogs. Share your work with your classmates.

8. Read Gibbons' *Spiders* and the make a big cut out of a spider. On each of
the spider's eight legs, write one unusual fact about spiders. Share your
work with your classmates.

9. Read Markle's *Outside and Inside Spiders* and do the "Looking Back"
activity on page 40. Share your answers with a classmate.

10. Read Charles' *Ugly Bug*. After reading, locate a field guide to insects in
your library. Choose a bug that you think could be called an ugly bug.
Draw a picture of the bug and write its name and two interesting facts
about it. Share your work with classmates.

11. Read pages 26 through 28 of Irvine's *Build It with Boxes*. Gather the
materials and follow the directions to make the fish. When you have
completed the project, bring it to school to share with classmates. You might
even think of a way to show a different animal in a different habitat.

12. Read pages 80 through 82 of Irvine's *Build It with Boxes*. Gather the
materials and make one of the animal masks shown in the book. Share
your finished project with your classmates.

LIFE SCIENCE—PLANTS

STUDENT OBJECTIVES

1. Identify different ways that seeds travel.
2. Identify the needs of plants.
3. Observe how sunlight and water affect growing plants.

RECOMMENDED READINGS

Ardley, Neil. *The Science Book of Things That Grow*. Harcourt Brace Jovanovich,
1991. (Objective 3)
This information book explains the mechanics of plant growth through simple
experiments.

Bunting, Eve. *Someday a Tree.* Illustrated by Ronald Himler. Clarion, 1993. (Objectives 1 & 2)
Alice is sad about the needless death of her favorite tree until she finds a hopeful solution.

Christensen, Bonnie. *An Edible Alphabet.* Dial Books, 1994. (Objective 1)
Wood engravings illustrate this alphabet book of unusual fruits and vegetables.

Ehlert, Lois. *Planting a Rainbow.* Harcourt Brace Jovanovich, 1988. (Objectives 2 & 3)
A mother and child plant a garden of colorful flowers.

Florian, Douglas. *Vegetable Garden.* Harcourt Brace Jovanovich, 1991. (Objectives 2 & 3)
A family's vegetable garden grows to maturity.

Gibbons, Gail. *From Seed to Plant.* Holiday House, 1991. (Objective 1)
This information book investigates seeds and the plants they produce.

Heller, Ruth. *The Reason for a Flower.* Grosset & Dunlap, 1983. (Objective 1)
This brilliantly illustrated book uses simple text to provide a wealth of plant information.

Herbert, Don. *Mr. Wizard's Supermarket Science.* Illustrated by Roy McKie. Random House, 1980. (Objectives 2 & 3)
This experiment book provides easy-to-follow experiments using household items.

Hiscock, Bruce. *The Big Tree.* Atheneum, 1991. (Objectives 1 & 3)
Hiscock chronicles the long life of a maple tree.

King, Elizabeth. *Backyard Sunflower.* Dutton Children's Books, 1993. (Objectives 2 & 3)
Samantha shares her adventures in her sunflower garden.

Markle, Sandra. *Outside and Inside Trees.* Macmillan, 1993. (Objectives 1, 2, & 3)
Beautiful photographs describe trees, how they survive, how they grow, and how they multiply.

Markmann, Erika. *Grow It! An Indoor/Outdoor Gardening Guide for Kids.* Illustrated by Gisela Konemund. Random House, 1991. (Objectives 2 & 3)
Markmann provides experiments and information for the growth and care of indoor and outdoor gardens.

Moore, Elaine. *Grandma's Garden.* Illustrated by Dan Andreasen. Lothrop, Lee & Shepard, 1994. (Objectives 2 & 3)
Kim and Grandma build their own special garden.

Muller, Gerda. *Around the Oak.* Dutton Children's Books, 1994. (Objective 1, 2, & 3)
Ben, Caroline, and Nick tour the forest to learn how it changes from season to season.

————. *The Garden in the City.* Dutton Children's Books, 1992. (Objectives 2 & 3)
After moving into a new home, a family plants a garden and watches it grow.

Owen, Cheryl. *My Nature Craft Book.* Photographs by Jonathan Pollack and Peter Cassidy. Illustrated by Stan North. Little, Brown and Company, 1993. (Objectives 1, 2, & 3)
This craft book uses materials found on the school playground to make a variety of items.

Shannon, George. *Seeds.* Illustrated by Steve Bjorkman. Houghton Mifflin, 1994. (Objective 2)
Shannon tells the story of a young boy's fascination with the neighbor's garden.

Sohi, Morteza E. *Look What I Did with a Leaf!* Walker and Company, 1993. (Objectives 1 & 3)
This craft book demonstrates creative and delightful ways to use a variety of leaves.

Walpole, Brenda. *175 Science Experiments to Amuse and Amaze Your Friends: Experiments! Tricks! Things to Make!* Illustrated by Kuo Kang Chen and Peter Bull. Random House, 1988. (Objective 3)
This experiment book covers a wide variety of topics, using easy-to-follow directions and valuable illustrations.

GROUP INTRODUCTORY ACTIVITY

Preparing for the Activity: Locate Ardley's *The Science Book of Things That Grow.* Have the following materials ready for each group: seeds, styrofoam cups, bottles of water, colored markers, and grid paper. A refrigerator or other dark place will be needed.

Focus: Read the experiment "Starting to Grow" from the book to the students. Follow the instructions for the experiment with the entire class. Place the plant in a sunny windowsill or under a grow light. Post the roster of your class and a piece of grid paper beside the plant. The students will take turns watering the experiment and charting the growth of the plant. Students will check their names off each time they are responsible for watering the plant and will date the line of the grid paper that indicates the growth of the plant. **Objective:** To satisfy the objectives of identifying the needs of plants and observing how sunlight and water affect growing plants, divide the students into groups and repeat the above experiment, changing the variables of water and sunlight. Have one group show what happens when the plant is given no water and another group show the effect of no sunlight. The data must be recorded for the same number of days in each of these experiments. After each group shares its data with the entire class, have students write theories about the effect of water and sunlight on the growth of plants.

Extending Activity: Divide the class into six groups. Each group will be responsible for one of the following experiments from the book: "Seed Needs," "Too Dark to Grow," "Plant Maze," "Brilliant Bean," "Clever Carrot," and "Indoor Garden." Provide each group with a worksheet that includes the following questions:

- What materials are needed?
- Who will bring the materials?
- How will data be recorded?
- How and where will the experiment be placed?
- How long will data be recorded?
- What are the results of the experiment?

The teacher will need to look at each individual experiment to determine the kind of data to be recorded.

Students will need help determining how to record data. Suggestions might include a bar graph or a list. Choose two days a week for the students to report to the entire class the progress of their experiment.

FOLLOW-UP ACTIVITIES FOR TEACHER AND STUDENTS TO SHARE

1. Read *Grow It! An Indoor/Outdoor Gardening Guide for Kids* by Erika Markmann. After experimenting and observing how the lack of light and water affect a plant, read the table of contents of this book, allowing the children to predict what the chapters are about. Then discuss the generalizations the class made about sunlight and read the chapter "Let There Be Light" to see if it agrees with the class' generalizations. Do the same with the chapter on watering. Use the other chapter titles to allow the students to predict what the book tells about the needs of plants. List their predictions, and then read the chapter to verify the predictions.

2. Before reading Ehlert's *Planting a Rainbow*, take students to a local green-house or florist. Have an adult volunteer serve as the recorder for the group. Have each student tell the recorder the name and color of their favorite flowering plant. After returning to the classroom, have the re-corder print all the colors on the list across the top of the chalkboard. Then read Ehlert's book and have students list under the proper color name both the flowers mentioned in Ehlert's book and the flowers seen on the field trip. Have students use library resources to determine whether their plant is an indoor or outdoor plant and its proper care. Provide students with a large white paper, crayons, and a pencil. Instruct students to make a mini poster of their favorite flower, including simple care instructions.

3. Secure the following items for this activity: four clay pots, one carrot, carrot seed, two avocado seeds, soil, a shallow dish, a tall glass, a knife, six toothpicks, and water. Read Florian's *Vegetable Garden* to the students. Have students try to grow both a carrot and an avacado from seed by planting the seeds in pots with soil. Have them also try rooting each plant from the top of a carrot and the seed of an avocado. The teacher will need to use the knife to cut the top off the carrot. The students can insert three toothpicks into the top of the carrot and into the avocado seed. The toothpicks allow students to immerse only the bottom half of the carrot top and the seed in a shallow dish or glass of water. Have students record their observations of the four plants in a daily log. After the avocado seed and carrot top have rooted, allow students to plant them in soil. Have students continue to compare and record observations of all four plants. After four to six weeks, have students graph the growth of the four plants and discuss their findings. Ask students the following questions:

   • Which plant grew fastest?
   • Which plant looks healthiest?
   • Which planting method worked best?

4. After reading Gibbons' *From Seed to Plant*, have students tell the six different methods of seed travel mentioned by the book. Write these methods on the board and have students choose one to act out. Have other students try to guess which one is being acted out. Have each student bring one seed to class. Make a class seed chart and identify each seed. Bring a large flower to class. Gather students together and talk about each of the different parts of the flower. Begin by pointing to the stem and asking students to name that part. Make labels for each part of the flower. Have these labels prepared for each student. Then have each student bring a flower to class. Work together to help students identify each part of the flower.

5. After reading Hiscock's *The Big Tree*, have the class create a timeline depicting the growth of the tree, beginning with how the seed arrived in 1775. At each date mentioned in the story, have students draw a picture of the tree and write a few sentences telling what was happening to the tree during that time period. For example, after six years, the big pine tree fell and allowed the seedling to get sunlight. Next, have students create a timeline for the seeds planted in the introductory activity. Display the seed timelines underneath the class timeline.

6. Read Heller's *The Reason for a Flower* to students. Discuss the parts of a flower using an actual flower as an exhibit. Then have each student bring a kind of food that has seeds in it. They might to choose to bring one that was mentioned in the book or a different item. After each student shows the food he or she brought, cut it open, display the seed(s), and let students sample the food. Bring a coconut to class and remind students that the coconut is the largest seed. Demonstrate to students how to drain the milk from the coconut; break it into pieces to share with students.

7. After reading *The Garden in the City* by Gerda Muller, ask the students to think about what plants they would want to plant in their own personal garden. Ask each student to develop and sketch a garden with specific plants in mind. On a separate sheet, each student should make two lists, one describing supplies needed and the other outlining responsibilities for care of the garden. Have each student present their plan to the class. Allow students to select one design to be used for a classroom garden. Then have students assign themselves to the responsibility and supply lists. Invite parents to participate in "A Gardening Extravaganza." This event will be to prepare the soil and plant the seeds for a class garden. Remember to invite parents back after the harvest for a tasting event. Parents can be asked to help make dips for the vegetables and to supply vegetable juices.

8. Prior to this activity, make a leaf animal using the examples in Sohi's *Look What I Did with a Leaf!* Take children to the playground or a nearby park to collect a variety of leaves. Ask each student to also bring 10 leaves from home. Read *Look What I Did with a Leaf!* and then show students the leaf animal example. Explain to students that they will be making a leaf mural and that each student will select an animal to make. They might choose one from the book or create one of their own. Then, using library resources, have each student identify at least two of the leaves used in their picture. Have each student add their leaf animal to the class mural.

9. Prior to this activity, collect a wide variety of gardening, seed, and plant catalogs. Read Shannon's *Seeds* to students and then have them discuss how Warren and Bill took care of the garden. List the things Warren will

need to take care of his garden. Students should determine why Warren and Bill named their plants "larkspur rabbits," "pink turtleheads," "monkey faces in the pansies," and "hens with little chicks." Explain to students that many plants have unusual names. Allow each student to browse through several plant catalogs to find an unusually named plant. Students should share the name and a picture of the plant with the class.

10. This project will take several months of warm weather to complete. Prior to reading King's *Backyard Sunflower*, buy a package of sunflower seeds at a nursery. Also buy a package of sunflower seeds at the grocery. Read King's book and allow each student to taste sunflower seeds from the grocery. Now select a spot in a remote area of the playground to plant a sunflower garden. Follow Samantha's planting and care suggestions. Create a classroom graph depicting the plants' growth by date.

11. Read Markle's *Outside and Inside Trees* and have a number of tree field guides available for students. After the reading, walk to a nearby tree. Have students look at the leaves and identify the tree using the field guides. Have students jot down the name of the tree. After returning to class, have students make a sketch of the tree, labeling specific parts, including seeds and leaves. Provide a place for students to display their work.

12. Read Bunting's *Someday a Tree* and then visit a local nursery with the students. Have the owner explain how to plant a tree and care for one. If possible, find tree seeds in an area near your school. (If there are no seeds in your area, plant a tree from fruit seeds, like an apple or peach, or plant a sapling.) Plant the seeds or sapling on the school ground and chart the growth of the tree or trees for the remainder of the school year.

13. Read Muller's *Around the Oak* and then take the students for a walk to the playground or a nearby park. As the class tours, have the students tell each other what plants they see. After returning to the classroom, divide the class into three groups and assign each group a season. Do not assign the current season. Each member of each group will need to draw a picture of how they think the area they visited might look in their assigned season. Have all students share and explain their pictures.

14. Read Moore's *Grandma's Garden* to students. Plant flower seeds in glass jars for residents of a local nursing home. Students should keep a daily log of the development of their plant. When the plants are flourishing, deliver them to the nursing home.

15. Share Christensen's *An Edible Alphabet* with students. Give each student an alphabet letter. Explain to students that they must match their alphabet letter with one way that a seed might travel. For example, "W" might stand for wind travel or "F" might stand for a seed traveling on an animal's fur. Students should illustrate their alphabet letters using a form of etch-

ing similar to Christensen's wood engravings. To emulate these wood engravings, students can make heavy crayon markings using a variety of colors to cover their entire sheet of white construction paper. Next, students should paint over the crayon with thick black tempera paint. Allow the students' paintings to dry overnight. The following day ask students to take a sharp object and etch the picture that accompanies the alphabet letter. The crayon will show through as areas are etched. Students should attach a brightly colored construction paper cut out of the alphabet letter to the finished picture using paste. Have students show and explain their pictures to other students.

FOLLOW-UP ACTIVITIES FOR INDIVIDUALS AND SMALL GROUPS

1. Using Sohi's *Look What I Did with a Leaf!* as a model, make a seed picture using a variety of seeds. Bean seeds, sunflower seeds, pumpkin seeds, and watermelon seeds are all possibilities. Attach seeds with glue to heavy paper or cardboard.

2. Read pages 22 and 23 of Walpole's *175 Science Experiments to Amuse and Amaze Your Friends: Experiments! Tricks! Things to Make!* Perform the experiment outlined on these pages to see how water travels upward from the roots of a plant.

3. Read page 162 of Walpole's *175 Science Experiments to Amuse and Amaze Your Friends: Experiments! Tricks! Things to Make!* Perform the experiment outlined on this page to see how green plants are affected by light.

4. Read page 33 of Herbert's *Mr. Wizard's Supermarket Science.* Perform the experiment described on this page. Each day, record the changes in the seeds by drawing pictures of them. Each week, take your experiment to school to share with classmates.

5. Read page 35 in Herbert's *Mr. Wizard's Supermarket Science.* Perform the experiment described on this page. After you have built your terrarium, bring it to school to share with classmates.

6. Read page 56 of Herbert's *Mr. Wizard's Supermarket Science.* Perform the experiment described on this page. After your sponge garden sprouts, take it to school to share with classmates.

7. Locate Owen's *My Nature Craft Book* and carefully look at a variety of the activities described in it. Select one item to make and bring to class when it is complete.

■

HUMAN BODY

STUDENT OBJECTIVES

1. Introduce students to body systems.
2. Identify the the areas of the Food Guide Pyramid.
3. Identify the elements of a diet that provide the human body with energy.
4. List substances that are harmful to the body.
5. Identify elements that help develop a healthy body.

RECOMMENDED READINGS

Ardley, Neil. *The Science Book of Sound.* Photography by Dave King. Harcourt Brace Jovanovich, 1991. (Objective 1)
This book of simple sound experiments relates the results to nature.

Barasch, Lynne. *Rodney's Inside Story.* Orchard, 1992. (Objective 2)
Baby Gray's adventures with vegetables and eating are described.

Berger, Melvin. *Germs Make Me Sick!* Illustrated by Marylin Hafner. HarperCollins, 1985. (Objective 4)
Using simple explanations and illustrations, this information book describes germs, their effects, and how the body fights against them.

Brown, Laurie Krasny, and Brown, Marc. *Dinosaurs Alive and Well: A Guide to Good Health.* Little, Brown and Company, 1990. (Objectives 1, 2, 3, & 4)
Dinosaurs present tips for healthy living.

Burningham, John. *Avocado Baby.* HarperCollins, 1982. (Objectives 2 & 3)
This fun story tells about a baby's love of avocados and how they help him grow.

Cole, Joanna. *The Magic School Bus: Inside the Human Body.* Illustrated by Bruce Degen. Scholastic, 1989. (Objective 1)
The Magic School Bus takes a tour of the human body.

————. *Your Insides.* Illustrated by Paul Meisel. Putnam & Grosset, 1992. (Objective 1)
This clever book introduces body systems and how they work.

Darling, David J. *Sounds Interesting: The Science of Acoustics*. Photographs from Union Stock Photos. Dillon Press, 1991. (Objective 1)
This information books provides explanations and experiments demonstrating how the ear and vocal cords work.

Emberley, Ed. *Ed Emberley's Great Thumbprint Drawing Book*. Little, Brown and Company, 1977. (Objective 1)
Emberley provides easy-to-follow models and directions for thumbprint art.

Herbert, Don. *Mr. Wizard's Supermarket Science*. Illustrated by Roy McKie. Random House, 1980. (Objective 1)
This experiment book describes easy-to-follow experiments that use household items.

Howe, James. *The Hospital Book*. Photographs by Mal Warshaw. Crown, 1981. (Objective 5)
Black-and-white photographs and text describe what happens when a child is ill and has to go to the hospital.

Kelley, True. *I've Got Chicken Pox*. Dutton Children's Books, 1994 (Objective 5)
Kelley provides students with all the stages of chicken pox and interesting facts about the disease.

Penrose, Gordon. *Dr. Zed's Science Surprises*. Simon and Schuster, 1989. (Objective 1)
Dr. Zed presents simple experiments for young learners.

Showers, Paul. *A Drop of Blood*. Illustrated by Don Madden. Thomas Y. Crowell, 1989. (Objective 1)
Clever pictures and text describe blood and its function in the body.

———. *How Many Teeth?* Illustrated by True Kelley. HarperCollins, 1991. (Objective 4)
Fun pictures and simple text follow Elizabeth and her family through the functioning and care of their teeth.

———. *What Happens to a Hamburger?* Illustrated by Anne Rockwell. Thomas Y. Crowell, 1985. (Objectives 1, 2, & 3)
This information book describes the digestive system and the importance of healthy eating.

———. *Your Skin and Mine*. Illustrated by Kathleen Kuchera. HarperCollins, 1991. (Objective 1)
This book uses simple text and illustrations to highlight the skin, its parts, its functions, and measures for its protection.

Suzuki, David, with Barbara Hehner. *Looking at the Body.* Illustrations by Nancy
Lou Reynolds. John Wiley & Sons, Inc., 1991. (Objective 1)
This information book couples an easy-to-understand narrative with investi-
gations for students to try.

What's on the Menu? Edited by Bobbye S. Goldstein. Illustrated by Chris L.
Demarest. Viking, 1992. (Objective 2)
This collection of delightful poems focuses on foods.

GROUP INTRODUCTORY ACTIVITY

Preparing for the Activity: Have available a variety of fruit pieces, making
sure that there is at least one piece for each student in the class. Allow time
for students to choose and begin eating a piece of the fruit. Then ask them to
tell what happens to the fruit as they eat it. Record their responses on a
chart.
Focus: Read Showers' *What Happens to a Hamburger?* to students. Throughout the reading, ask students to participate in the experiments that Showers
provides. Have students compare their observations on eating fruit to the
information in the book. Explain to students that the digestive system is just
one of several body systems; ask if they can name other body systems.
Objective: To satisfy the objective of introducing students to body systems,
students will create body system "murals." Locate Cole's *Your Insides.* Prepare
four child-sized outlines of the human body on kraft paper for this project.
The easiest way to do this is to trace a student in the class. Attach these
outlines to walls in the classroom and then read *Your Insides.* Label each outline as follows: Muscles and Bones, Heart and Lungs, Stomach and Intes-
tines, and Brain and Nerves. Divide the class into pairs and have each pair
select a part of the body they would like to recreate for the mural. Provide
students with construction paper, ribbon, glue, string, fabric scraps, paper
clips, straws, and other collage materials. Pictures from encyclopedias may be
helpful to students in recreating the body part. Attach finished parts to the
appropriate body mural. Explain to students that these murals represent some
of the body systems of all humans.
Extending Activity: Have each pair of students show their piece of the body
system map and then point to the area of their own bodies where this part is
located. Each pair of students should explain the function of that part of the
system to the class. Conclude by sharing Cole's *The Magic School Bus: Inside
the Human Body.*

FOLLOW-UP ACTIVITIES FOR
TEACHER AND STUDENTS TO SHARE

1. Share Barasch's *Rodney's Inside Story* and then have students list all the foods mentioned in this story. Allow each child to name a vegetable that will be used to make a class stew. If possible, visit a local grocery or farmer's market to buy ingredients for vegetable stew. A simple stew can be made using a crock pot, chicken broth, water, barley, seasonings, and a variety of vegetables. As students are eating their stew, have them share why they selected their vegetable.

2. Read several of the poems in *What's on the Menu?* to students. Form the class into pairs and have each pair select their favorite poem and identify the foods mentioned in that poem. Each pair should use library resources to determine where their food would be placed in the Food Guide Pyramid. Ask students to search their kitchen cabinets for a food item that contains one food mentioned in their poem and to bring the item to share with the class. Ask students to work in groups to create a giant mural representation of the Food Guide Pyramid. Have them write the foods from their poems on the mural.

3. Before sharing Showers' *Your Skin and Mine*, provide each student with a magnifying glass. Allow them five minutes to look at their skin through the magnifying glass. Then ask students to describe what they saw. After reading the book, have students look at a classmate and list all of her or his observable body parts that are skin. Do a variety of the activities that Showers suggests. Have students create pictures using their fingerprints. The simplest way to do this activity is to use an ink pad. Provide students with posterboard, markers, old magazines, scissors, and glue. Explain to students that they may use these materials to create a poster illustrating at least two ways to take care of their epidermis.

4. Share Berger's *Germs Make Me Sick!* and have students generate a list of where they might get germs in their everyday life. Write the students' responses on the board. Create another list of ways the body helps protect itself against these germs. Ask students to create short acrostic poems using one of the words from the lists they have generated. For example, if "wash" was one of the words, the poem might read:

> Washing
> All the time,
> Soap
> Helps.

Ask students to illustrate their poems and then display the poems in the classroom.

5. Prior to this activity, cut out a small dinosaur shape for each student using bright construction paper. Read the Browns' *Dinosaurs Alive and Well: A Guide to Good Health* and ask students to share one of the tips from the book aloud. Ask each student to explain why this tip is important for healthy living and to write down the tip on the dinosaur. After each child has shared and recorded a tip, display the dinosaurs on a bulletin board already entitled, "Dinosaurs for Health." Ask students if they can think of other tips for healthy living. Add these to the board. Provide every student with 10 half-sheets of paper that are stapled together like a book. On the top of each sheet, write the following words: "For healthy living, today I...." Explain to students that they will use these sheets to keep a Healthy Living Journal for the next 10 days. During the last 10 minutes of each day, have students write in their journals. At the end of the 10-day period, ask each student to share one entry with the class.

6. Read Showers' *A Drop of Blood* and then ask students to work in pairs to draw an outline on white kraft paper of each other's bodies. Following the drawing on page 15 of Showers' book, have students design the way blood moves through their bodies by using red yarn, red crayons, glue, and a red construction paper heart. Display this body art along the halls of the school.

7. After sharing Showers' *How Many Teeth?*, have a dentist or dental hygienist visit the classroom to explain proper brushing and flossing techniques to students. For a fun activity, have students make crazy teeth-print pictures. Give each student a 4" x 5" piece of white construction paper on which they can bite down and leave an imprint of their teeth. Then ask them to use a colored pencil to lightly shade the area of the bite imprint. From this beginning, students can make their bite print into a design or picture. Display the pictures in the classroom.

8. Introduce Darling's *Sounds Interesting: The Science of Acoustics* by reading pages 23 through 31 and pages 40 and 41 to the students. Now, reread each experiment to the class, asking for volunteers to demonstrate each experiment. Give students ample practice time and proper materials. Have each group of volunteers demonstrate and explain their experiment.

9. Before sharing Howe's *The Hospital Book*, contact a local hospital to plan a class field trip. To help prepare for this trip, read Howe's book to students. Divide students into groups and ask each group to come up with five questions they would like to ask on their hospital visit. Next, bring all the groups together and have each group share their questions with the class, writing all the questions on the board. Delete any duplicate questions and add any questions to areas that might have been missed.

Allow the class to select five to ten questions they are especially interested in. Write each question on a 3" x 5" card. Give each group one or two questions to ask during the visit to the hospital; have the group record the answers they receive to their questions. Upon returning from the hospital, allow students to write and illustrate their questions and answers on a sheet of white construction paper. Compile the sheets into a class book and display.

10. After sharing Burningham's *Avocado Baby*, ask students why they think this story could not possibly be true. What other kinds of food would the baby need to grow big and strong? Provide each child with an 8½" x 11" sheet of white paper with a large triangle shape drawn in the middle. Draw a large triangle shape on the chalkboard and have the entire class help make a copy of the Food Guide Pyramid. Tell students that this pyramid shows all the different foods they need to eat every day to become strong and healthy. Ask students what foods the baby in the story needed to add to his diet to become strong and healthy. Have students think about what foods they need to add to their daily food intake to remain healthy. Ask children to write down what they had for breakfast or lunch and then record beside each food what groups of the Food Guide Pyramid they have already eaten that day. Students can then decide what groups they need to eat from. Have students take their Food Guide Pyramids home to put on their refrigerators as a reminder of what they should be eating every day.

11. Before sharing Kelley's *I've Got Chicken Pox*, ask students who have had chicken pox to briefly tell what they remember the most about it. After reading the story, share the "Pox Facts" at the bottom of each page with students. Make a class chart showing how many students in the class have had chicken pox. Then have students choose another ailment that interests them. Provide some examples, including colds, flu, asthma, and diabetes. Explain to students that they need to find several interesting facts about the ailment they have chosen. Allow time for them to share with class.

FOLLOW-UP ACTIVITIES FOR INDIVIDUALS AND SMALL GROUPS

1. Read pages 10 and 11 of Ardley's *The Science Book of Sound*. Practice the experiment demonstrating how the ear detects sound and show the experiment to your classmates.

2. Find a partner for this activity. Read page 18 of Ardley's *The Science Book of Sound*. Practice the experiment demonstrating how to hear a heartbeat and show the experiment to your classmates.

3. Read page 19 of Ardley's *The Science Book of Sound*. Practice the experiment demonstrating how to make your voice louder and show the experiment to your classmates.

4. After finding a partner, read pages 6 through 11 of Suzuki's *Looking at the Body*. Do the two activities on your body and share the results of the first activity with your classmates. After you have practiced the second activity, teach this game to your whole class.

5. You will need a partner for this activity. Read pages 18 through 21 and pages 24 through 25 of Suzuki's *Looking at the Body*. Do the fingerprint activity on pages 24 and 25 with your partner. After practicing with your partner, demonstrate this activity for your class and allow classmates to participate.

6. Find a partner and then read page 59 of Herbert's *Mr. Wizard's Supermarket Science*. Follow the directions on this page to make a stethoscope. After you have listened to each other's heartbeats, try to find those of your classmates.

7. Find a partner for this activity. Read page 12 in Penrose's *Dr. Zed's Science Surprises* and try the activities outlined on this page on body movement. After you and your partner have practiced, teach these tricks to your classmates.

8. Find a partner for this activity. Read page 15 in Penrose's *Dr. Zed's Science Surprises* and try the activities outlined on this page to test your tastebuds. After you and your partner have tried this experiment, demonstrate your findings for your classmates.

9. Locate a copy of *Ed Emberley's Great Thumbprint Drawing Book*. Try several of his thumbprint designs and create some of your own. Share your pictures with classmates.

10. After completing your research for Kelley's *I've Got Chicken Pox*, try to find someone who has had the ailment you researched. If they are willing, set up an interview with them about the ailment and report your findings to the class.

■

EARTH SCIENCE

STUDENT OBJECTIVES

1. Describe the earth's surface as being composed of rocks, soil, and water.
2. Describe the differences in the communities of life in salt water and fresh water.

3. Recognize the elements of weather: temperature, clouds, wind, and water.

4. Describe and explain a variety of weather conditions, including snow, rain, hail, tornadoes, hurricanes, floods, and droughts.

RECOMMENDED READINGS

Albert, Burton. *Windsongs and Rainbows*. Illustrated by Susan Stillman. Simon & Schuster, 1993. (Objectives 3 & 4)
Beautiful text and pictures describe how the senses respond to weather.

Baylor, Byrd. *Everybody Needs a Rock*. Illustrated by Peter Parnall. Scribners, 1974. (Objective 1)
Baylor's imagery beautifully describes the need for a special rock.

Brandenberg, Aliki. *My Visit to the Aquarium*. HarperCollins, 1993. (Objective 2)
A child takes the reader to an aquarium to see both saltwater and freshwater communities.

Branley, Franklyn M. *Rain & Hail*. Illustrated by Harriett Barton. HarperCollins, 1983. (Objective 4)
A clear text simply describes rain and hail.

———. *Snow Is Falling*. Illustrated by Holly Keller. Thomas Y. Crowell, 1986. (Objective 4)
This information book explains and describes snow.

Carson, Jo. *The Great Shaking*. Illustrated by Robert Andrew Parker. Orchard, 1994. (Objective 1)
A bear describes the earthquakes of 1811 and 1812 in New Madrid, Missouri.

Cech, John. *First Snow, Magic Snow*. Illustrated by Sharon McGinley-Nally. FourWinds, 1992. (Objectives 3 & 4)
Cech bases his book on a Russian folktale that describes Grandfather Frost and his granddaughter Snowflake.

Conover, Chris. *Sam Panda and Thunder Dragon*. Farrar, Straus and Giroux, 1992. (Objectives 3 & 4)
Sam Panda and Thunder Dragon are at first only fair-weather friends, but then Thunder Dragon delivers the rain.

Dewey, Ariane. *The Sky*. Green Tiger Press, 1993. (Objectives 3 & 4)
This beautifully illustrated book presents a realistic and magical look at the sky.

Drake, Jane, and Love, Ann. *The Kid's Summer Handbook.* Illustrated by Heather Collins. Ticknor & Fields, 1994. (Objective 1)
This activity guide provides wonderful ideas for children to try.

Gans, Roma. *Rock Collecting.* Illustrated by Holly Keller. HarperCollins, 1984. (Objective 1)
This information book outlines rocks and rock collecting.

Gibbons, Gail. *Weather Forecasting.* Aladdin, 1987. (Objectives 3 & 4)
Gibbons describes how weather forecasters predict and track weather conditions.

————. *Weather Words and What They Mean.* Holiday House, 1990. (Objectives 3 & 4)
Gibbons provides simple text and illustrations to explain weather phenomena.

Ketteman, Helen. *The Year of No More Corn.* Illustrated by Robert Andrew Parker. Orchard Books, 1993. (Objectives 3 & 4)
A farmer tells of all the mishaps that befell his 1928 corn crop.

Killion, Bette. *The Same Wind.* Illustrated by Barbara Bustetter Falk. HarperCollins, 1992. (Objectives 3 & 4)
A girl asks the wind that she enjoys if it is same wind that causes weather changes.

McKissack, Patricia C. *Mirandy and Brother Wind.* Illustrated by Jerry Pinkney. Alfred A. Knopf, 1988. (Objectives 3 & 4)
Mirandy asks Brother Wind to help her win the cake walk.

Murphy, Bryan. *Experiment with Water.* Lerner, 1991. (Objective 3)
This experiment book describes the many ways that water is a force in our everyday lives.

Parker, Steve. *Rocks and Minerals.* Dorling Kindersley, 1993. (Objective 1)
This handbook for young students describes a variety of rocks and minerals.

Shaw, Charles G. *It Looked Like Spilt Milk.* Harper & Row, 1947. (Objectives 3 & 4)
Simple text and illustrations depict how cloud formations look to an observer.

Singer, Marilyn. *Sky Words.* Illustrated by Deborah Kogan Ray. Macmillan, 1994. (Objective 3)
Weather concepts are brought alive through illustrations and poetry.

Turner, Ann. *A Moon for Seasons.* Illustrated by Robert Noreika. Macmillan, 1994. (Objectives 3 & 4)
Beautiful poems and illustrations describe each season.

Walpole, Brenda. *175 Science Experiments to Amuse and Amaze Your Friends: Experiments! Tricks! Things to Make!* Illustrated by Kuo Kang Chen and Peter Bull. Random House, 1988. (Objectives 3 & 4)
This experiment book covers a wide variety of topics with easy-to-follow directions and valuable illustrations.

Weather. Poems selected by Lee Bennett Hopkins. Illustrations by Melanie Hall. HarperCollins, 1994. (Objectives 3 & 4)
Hopkins has selected delightful poems about all types of weather.

Weeks, Sarah. *Hurricane City.* Illustrations by James Warhola. HarperCollins, 1993. (Objectives 3 & 4)
A family in Hurricane City describes the wide array of hurricanes that have blasted through their city.

Whittington, Mary K. *Winter's Child.* Illustrated by Sue Ellen Brown. Atheneum, 1992. (Objectives 3 & 4)
Winter discovers a baby lying in the snow—the Baby Spring.

Zolotow, Charlotte. *The Seashore Book.* Illustrations by Wendell Minor. HarperCollins, 1992. (Objective 2)
Zolotow describes what might be found on the seashore.

Zweifel, Frances. *The Make-Something Club.* Illustrated by Ann Schweninger. Viking, 1994. (Objective 1)
This fun activity book has creative ideas for each month of the year.

GROUP INTRODUCTORY ACTIVITY

Preparing for the Activity: The week before officially starting a weather unit, read the following books to students: Cech's *First Snow, Magic Snow,* Whittington's *Winter's Child,* Conover's *Sam Panda and Thunder Dragon,* and McKissack's *Mirandy and Brother Wind.* After each reading, have students list the weather phenomenon described in the story. After reading Cech's *First Snow, Magic Snow,* ask students, "In this story, what caused the snow? Is this what really causes snow?" After reading Conover's *Sam Panda and Thunder Dragon,* ask students, "In this story, why did it rain? Is this really what makes it rain?" Ask similar questions after sharing the other two books.

Focus: Divide students into small groups. Have each group create make-believe explanations for one of these weather phenomena: hail, tornadoes, hurricanes, sleet, fog, floods, and droughts. Remind students to make their explanations as fun and silly as possible. Provide students several class sessions to generate their work and allow them time to share their finished products with the entire class. When the make-believe explanations are complete, explain to students that in the next few class sessions they will find out how these phenomena really happen.

Objective: To satisfy the objectives of recognizing the elements of weather and describing a variety of weather conditions, have students fully describe what really happens during their previously chosen weather phenomenon. Share Gibbons' *Weather Words and What They Mean* with students. Each group should create a poster illustrating how and why the weather event occurs. Students will need to have access to a variety of reference materials on weather. Each group will also need markers and poster board. Have the groups share their posters with the class.

Extending Activity: Have each student write a journal about the weather phenomenon they have studied. For example, if the student has been studying snow, the journal entries might be about being stranded in the snow or being in a blizzard. Journal entries might include:

- Safety precautions they might take in the storm
- Conditions of pets
- What might happen to their home
- How they would communicate with others
- What they might do to stay warm

Allow time for each student to share a part of her or his journal with a classmate.

FOLLOW-UP ACTIVITIES FOR
TEACHER AND STUDENTS TO SHARE

1. Take students to the playground or a nearby park and read Shaw's *It Looked Like Spilt Milk*. Then provide each student with drawing paper, a firm drawing surface, and charcoal pencils or pastels. Let the students draw what they see in the clouds. After returning to the classroom, share Dewey's *The Sky*. Allow students to share their drawings with one another. Each student will need to make her or his own 10-page booklet using this drawing as the cover for a cloud diary. For the cloud diary, have students observe the clouds from a classroom window or the playground. After each day's observation, send several students to the library to research the cloud types they observed. Each day students should date their diary page, sketch the cloud formation they observed, and indicate its name. At the end of the two-week period, have students determine if there were any types of clouds that were not observed during this time frame and have students graph the number of times they saw each type of cloud. Display the diaries in the library.

2. After reading Killion's *The Same Wind*, ask students to determine the other elements of weather—temperature, clouds, and water. Have students create acrostic poems using the four elements of weather. Their poems should reflect how each element affects the weather. Have students illustrate their poem using tempera paints. Provide the following example of an acrostic poem using the word "wind":

> Wild
> Icy
> Noisy
> Dancing

3. Read the following sections of Murphy's *Experiment with Water*, to the students: "Water All Around Us," "The Water Cycle," and "Water and the Weather." Have pairs of students perform the experiment provided in the section entitled "The Water Cycle." Each experiment should be set up in a different area of the classroom. Have students record results for five days and then have them graph and compare results. Ask the following questions:

   - Which container had the least amount of water by the end of the experiment and why?
   - Which container had the most and why?

4. After reading Zolotow's *The Seashore Book*, have students generate a list of things found in a saltwater environment such as the seashore. Then have students generate a list of things found in a freshwater environment such as a lake or pond. Have students recreate a small freshwater environment in the classroom. This can easily be done with a 10- to 20-gallon aquarium and help from a local pet store. This would be an appropriate time to visit a local aquarium, pond, lake, ocean, or even a pet store specializing in aquatic life.

5. After reading Aliki's *My Visit to the Aquarium*, divide students into two groups—the Saltwater Community and the Freshwater Community. Explain to students that their task is to recreate their water community in a corner of their classroom. Tell students they will be making a huge mural/collage of their habitat and remind them to include the appropriate animal and plant life. Provide students with wall-sized mural paper, paints, markers, colored pencils, fabric scraps, construction paper, and a variety of collage materials. Give each group of students a week to complete their habitat murals. Then provide time for each group to present their habitats to the other students in the class and other classrooms. Have them include in their presentations information regarding types of plant

and animal life, location of their habitat around the world, and any unique facts about their habitat.

6. Share Gibbons' *Weather Forecasting* with students. Discuss the jobs that weather forecasters do. Have students keep a daily log of the temperature while working on this unit. The temperature should be recorded at the same time each day. Have students listen to the daily weather report to find the record low and high temperatures for each day. Have students create simple bar graphs to compare their daily findings with the record highs and lows.

7. Prior to this activity, prepare materials for a weather trivia event by printing the following on 3" x 5" cards:

   • Where did the most rain occur in 1 minute and how much fell?

   • Where did the most rain occur in 24 hours and how much fell?

   • Where did the most rain occur in 12 months and how much fell?

   • Where did the most snow fall in 24 hours and how much fell?

   • Where did the most snow fall in 1 month and how much fell?

   • What location has the most rainy days in a year?

   • Which state has the most rainfall?

   • Where did the largest hailstone fall in the United States and how much did it weigh?

   Share Branley's *Snow Is Falling* and *Rain & Hail* with students. Divide the class into pairs and give each pair one of the index cards. Ask them to use library resources to find the answers. Have students share their questions and answers with the class. Pairs with the same questions may find different answers depending on the source. Be sure to have students give their resource.

8. Read Gans' *Rock Collecting* and have students bring their favorite rock from home. Using library sources, determine the name of each rock and facts relating to the rock. Give each student a 5" x 8" index card and have them print on it the name of their rock and several facts about their rock. Facts might include where this kind of rock is found, how hard the rock is, what the rock is used for, what it is made of or its origin, and what colors it can be. Display all rocks and fact cards in a class rock collection. Invite other students to view the collection.

9. Turner's *A Moon for Seasons* contains poems about each season. Each section contains poems that describe the moon, animal behavior, characteristics of plants, and weather changes during that particular season. The teacher could begin each new season with this activity or divide the class into four groups and do the activity one time during the school year.

Discuss with students things that are unique to that season and list their responses on the board under the specific season. Prepare four cut outs, one representing each season. Place these cut outs around the classroom, marking the following categories on each cut out: Moon, Weather, Plants, and Animals. Read the poems for each season and have students add to their list on their particular cut out.

10. Read pages 196 and 197 of Drake and Love's *The Kid's Summer Handbook* and then take a rock walk with the class. Have students collect rocks and then provide them with glue and paint to make a rock sculpture. Have students identify the type of rock used in their sculpture. Use field guides from the library to help with identification. Ask students to name their sculpture using the name of the rock, e.g., Giant Granite Giraffe. Display the rock art in the school library. Culminate this activity by reading Baylor's *Everybody Needs a Rock*.

11. Prior to reading Carson's *The Great Shaking*, ask students if they know what causes an earthquake. Write their responses on the board. Explain that they will be listening to a story about a bear's account of an earthquake that took place in 1811 and 1812 in New Madrid, Missouri. Read the story to students and talk about the bear's account. Ask students if they think the bear understands what caused the earthquake. Read the "Note About Earthquakes" on the last page of the book and have each child write an account of what a real earthquake might be like from a human's point of view. Ask if any students have been in an earthquake. Allow those students to write about their experience. Ask students to share their accounts with the class.

12. Share a variety of poems from *Weather* with students. Be sure to include some poems from each season. If you live in a part of the country that does not experience all four seasons, have pictures on hand that visually describe the seasons. Then ask students to select a season they would like to illustrate through poetry. They will need to think about the type of weather that occurs during that season. Allow time for students to share their poems with the class.

13. Share several poems from Singer's *Sky Words*, including the one entitled "When the Tornado Came." Write the following list on the chalkboard and ask students to select a weather condition to write about: Fog, Rain, Hurricane, Snow, Sleet, and Blizzard. Next, ask students to think how this weather condition might affect one kind of animal. Ask students to write a poem or a paragraph about their weather condition from this animal's point of view. Share the writings with the class.

14. Before sharing Weeks' *Hurricane City*, ask students if they know how hurricanes are named. Allow time for discussion. After the reading, ask students to find out if there is an important hurricane named after them-

selves or any of their family members. Provide almanacs to help students do their research. Have students share two facts they learned about their namesake hurricane with the class. If any students have been in a hurricane, allow them to report on their experience.

15. Before sharing Albert's *Windsongs and Rainbows*, divide the class into eight groups. Provide each group with a piece of chart tablet that has the following phrases written across the top:

- When I hear the wind, I hear:
- When I feel the wind, I feel:
- When I see the wind, I see:
- When I hear the rain, I hear:
- When I feel the rain, I feel:
- When I see the rain, I see:
- When I feel the sun, I feel:
- When I see the sun, I see:

Each chart paper will have only one line written across the top. Instruct each group to write down their ideas on their paper. Provide about 10 to 15 minutes for students to work on their paper. Have one student from each group bring the paper to the front of the class. Display their papers across the chalkboard. Then have some time to share from each paper. Read Albert's book, having students listen carefully for the things included in the book that were also on their list. After sharing, add to the list things from the book that were not previously included.

16. After reading Ketteman's *The Year of No More Corn*, have students list all the different kinds of weather that affected the corn crop and what effect the different kinds of weather had on the corn crop. Then ask students to think of another profession and how that profession is affected by the weather. The teacher might suggest some of the following professions for consideration: firefighter, mail carrier, construction worker, and roofer. After the students have chosen a profession to consider, allow them 10 minutes to write down all the ways that different kinds of weather might affect their job. Provide time for students to share their ideas with classmates.

FOLLOW-UP ACTIVITIES FOR INDIVIDUALS AND SMALL GROUPS

1. Select a small group of friends to help you with this activity. Read Conover's *Sam Panda and Thunder Dragon* aloud to your group. Create a short play that depicts the story. Make costumes using old material, paint,

and construction paper. Assign each group member a part in the performance. You may write each cast member's lines on an index card for them to use during the performance. Act out your play for your class.

2. Read Murphy's *Experiment with Water* and select one experiment not done by your class to demonstrate for other students. Be sure to ask your teacher to approve the experiment you choose.

3. Reread Gibbons' *Weather Forecasting*. Watch several different weather forecasters and explain to classmates why you like one better than another.

4. Read page 15 of Walpole's *175 Science Experiments to Amuse and Amaze Your Friends: Experiments! Tricks! Things to Make!*. Follow the directions on this page for constructing a rain gauge. Keep a chart showing the amount of rainfall for one month. Share your chart with classmates at the end of the month.

5. Read pages 78 and 79 of Walpole's *175 Science Experiments to Amuse and Amaze Your Friends: Experiments! Tricks! Things to Make!* Follow the directions on these pages for constructing a wind vane. Keep a daily chart telling from which direction the wind is blowing. Also record the weather for that day. Try to determine if there is any correlation between the direction from which the wind is blowing and any changes in the weather. Share your results with classmates.

6. Read pages 18 and 19 of Zweifel's *The Make-Something Club*. Follow the directions on these pages to make pet rocks. Be sure to use your favorite rocks. Share your new pets with your classmates.

7. Read pages 34 and 35 of Parker's *Rocks and Minerals*. These pages will help you understand how rocks leave records of time. Follow the directions on page 35 to make an anticline. Share and explain your model with the class.

■

SPACE

STUDENT OBJECTIVES

1. Describe the motion of the earth and relate how it determines day and night.

2. Define the word "constellations" and give examples of the pictures the stars make in the night sky.

3. Identify the nine planets in our solar system.

RECOMMENDED READINGS

Bradman, Tony. *It Came from Outer Space.* Illustrated by Carol Wright. Dial, 1992. (Objective 3)
Bradman's surprise ending provides students with a different outlook on aliens.

Branley, Franklyn M. *The Moon Seems to Change.* Illustrated by Barbara and Ed Emberley. HarperCollins, 1987. (Objective 1)
This information book provides a clear understanding of the phases of the moon.

―――. *The Sky Is Full of Stars.* Illustrated by Felicia Bond. HarperCollins, 1983. (Objective 2)
This factual book presents information about constellations.

―――. *What Makes Day and Night?* Illustrated by Arthur Dorros. HarperCollins, 1986. (Objective 1)
This simple information book clearly explains what causes day and night.

Carlstrom, Nancy White. *Who Gets the Sun Out of Bed?* Illustrated by David McPhail. Little, Brown and Company, 1992. (Objective 1)
Carlstrom and McPhail provide readers with an excellent portrayal of a sleepy sun.

Cherry, Lynne. *The Armadillo from Amarillo.* Harcourt Brace & Company, 1994. (Objective 1)
An armadillo searches for his place in the universe.

Cole, Joanna. *The Magic School Bus Lost in the Solar System.* Illustrated by Bruce Degen. Scholastic, 1992. (Objective 3)
The Magic School Bus finds its way through the solar system.

Drake, Jane, and Love, Ann. *The Kid's Summer Handbook.* Illustrated by Heather Collins. Ticknor & Fields, 1994. (Objective 2)
This activity guide provides wonderful ideas for children to try.

Gibbons, Gail. *The Planets.* Holiday House, 1993. (Objective 3)
This information book describes the characteristics of the nine planets.

―――. *Stargazers.* Holiday House, 1992. (Objective 2)
Gibbons provides a brief yet thorough explanation of stars and stargazing.

Goble, Paul. *The Lost Children: The Boys Who Were Neglected.* Bradbury Press. 1993. (Objective 2)
A Blackfoot Indian legend explains the origin of the Pleiades stars.

Herbert, Don. Mr. *Wizard's Supermarket Science.* Illustrated by Roy McKie. Random House, 1980. (Objective 2)
This experiment book provides easy-to-follow experiments that use household items.

Hirst, Robin, and Hirst, Sally. *My Place in Space.* Illustrated by Roland Harvey with Joe Levine. Orchard, 1988. (Objective 3)
By relating a person's address to the universe, this playful book provides an illustration of the broadness of our universe.

Irvine, Joan. *Build It with Boxes.* Illustrated by Linda Hendry. Morrow Junior Books, 1993. (Objective 1)
Irvine describes many fun projects to make with boxes.

Kitamura, Satoshi. *UFO Diary.* Farrar Straus Giroux, 1989. (Objective 3)
A UFO takes a wrong turn and lands on Earth.

Lauber, Patricia. *How We Learned the Earth Is Round.* Illustrated by Meagan Lloyd. Harper Trophy, 1990. (Objective 1)
This excellent information book explains the various theories of the Earth's shape—from flat to round.

Leedy, Loreen. *Postcards from Pluto: A Tour of the Solar System.* Holiday House, 1993. (Objective 3)
Dr. Quasar takes children on a tour of the nine planets.

Oughton, Jerrie. *How the Stars Fell into the Sky.* Illustrated by Lisa Desinini. Houghton Mifflin, 1992. (Objective 2)
This Navajo legend explains the stars' patterns in the sky.

Pinkwater, Daniel. *Guys from Space.* Aladdin Books, 1992. (Objective 3)
When a spaceship lands in his backyard, a boy visits another planet.

Robinson, Fay. *Space Probes to the Planets.* Albert Whitman & Company, 1993. (Objective 3)
This excellent fact book on space describes space probes and planets.

Rosen, Sidney. *Which Way to the Milky Way?* Illustrated by Dean Lindberg. Carolrhoda, 1992. (Objective 3)
This question-and-answer book provides information about galaxies.

Stott, Carole. *Night Sky.* Dorling Kindersley, Inc., 1993. (Objectives 2 & 3)
This excellent handbook explains how to look at the sky and what to look for.

GROUP INTRODUCTORY ACTIVITY

Preparing for the Activity: Locate Gibbons' *The Planets* and Leedy's *Postcards from Pluto: A Tour of the Solar System*. Each student will need her or his home address, a 5" x 8" piece of sturdy cardstock, a pen, and markers.

Focus: Before reading, tell students that they each will select their favorite planet and write a letter from that planet to their parents. They will need to listen to the readings for information about their planet because the descriptions of the planets in their letters should be clear enough to enable their parents to guess which planet their child is on.

Objective: To satisfy the objective of identifying the nine planets, have students list characteristics of each of the planets. To prepare for this part of the activity, write the names of the planets across the top of the board. As students tell characteristics of each planet, record their ideas on the chalkboard.

Extending Activity: Have each student select her or his favorite planet and create an illustrated postcard to send to parents. Each postcard should include several facts about the selected planet. Use the examples in Leedy's book to help students with their postcards. After the cards are mailed, ask students if their parents guessed which planet they were writing from. Culminate this activity by sharing Cole's *The Magic School Bus Lost in the Solar System*.

FOLLOW-UP ACTIVITIES FOR
TEACHER AND STUDENTS TO SHARE

1. After sharing Bradman's *It Came from Outer Space*, divide the class into eight groups, one for each of the planets, excluding Earth. Have each group make an illustrated instruction manual for an earthling coming to visit their planet. This manual might include how to dress, what they would find to eat, how they would breathe, how they would communicate, what they would drink, and whether or not they would be weightless. Each group should share their manual with classmates.

2. After reading Carlstrom's *Who Gets the Sun Out of Bed?*, have students make a list of the things that could not get the sun out of bed and the two things that could get the sun out of bed (moon, midnight). Using encyclopedias, have students research why the moon and midnight help the sun come up.

3. This activity would make a good follow-up to Carlstrom's *Who Gets the Sun Out of Bed?* Read Branley's *What Makes Day and Night?* and ask students to work in pairs to select a particular time of day or night. Provide each pair with a large piece of paper (2' x 3'), old magazines, scissors, glue, crayons, and markers. Ask students to cut out magazine pictures depicting activities that might occur during the time of day they have

selected. Have students attach their cut outs to the large sheet of paper in collage fashion. Under their collage, students should draw a picture showing how the sun and earth would look at the time of day their pictures represent. Each group should explain their collage to the class.

4. Share Branley's *The Moon Seems to Change*, being sure to have students perform the experiment on pages 20 through 26. Have students create a cover for their Moon Diary, making available heavy construction paper, markers, sequins, glitter, foil, scissors, and glue for this activity. Each student should have seven pages of paper in his or her diary. Ask students to look at the moon every night for two weeks. They will need to draw and record what they see. It would be helpful to send a note home prior to this activity explaining its purpose. Each morning, provide time for students to share their observations from the previous night. Display the diaries in the school library at the close of this activity.

5. Before reading Gibbons' *Stargazers*, provide each student with a letter of the alphabet written or typed on a sheet of paper. Tell students they will be listening for words that begin with their letter. As they listen to the story, students should list words on their paper. After the reading, have students choose one of their words to be used as an entry for their letter in a class ABC book about the stars. For example, A could stand for Astronomers, B for Black Hole, C for Constellation, etc. Students should illustrate and write one fact given in Gibbons' book for their page in the class book.

6. After sharing Pinkwater's *Guys from Space*, divide the class into four groups. Provide each group with a set of eight sentence strips. Instruct each group to write down eight events that took place in the story, put their sentence strips in the correct order, and share them with the entire class. Next, give each group another set of blank sentence strips and instruct them to make up their own story similar to Pinkwater's, except this time they will travel to another planet and have a different experience. Students will need to use the library media center for research to create their stories. Allow each group time to act out its new story for the class. Students may need to bring props from home.

7. Begin this activity by sharing Branley's *The Sky Is Full of Stars*, Goble's *The Lost Children: The Boys Who Were Neglected*, and Oughton's *How the Stars Fell into the Sky*. Ask students to select their favorite constellation. You will need a variety of books and encyclopedias on stars to help students make their selections. After selections are made, give students the following materials: a sheet of 11" x 17" paper; yellow, white, silver, and gold crayons; dark blue or black watercolor or diluted dark blue or black tempera paint; and paintbrushes. Have students draw their constellation on the paper with the crayons. Have them paint over their paper with the paint. Allow the paper to dry and display it on the ceiling of the

classroom. Another activity that students might enjoy is creating their constellation by punching out its design on a piece of paper. To do this, hold the paper in front of a light source in a darkened classroom so that the pattern is shown on a wall. An overhead projector or large flashlight can be used as a light source. Directions for a similar activity are provided on page 30 of Branley's book.

8. Read Rosen's *Which Way to the Milky Way?* to students. Provide each student with a brad, glue, scissors, yellow and dark blue tempera or watercolor, sequins, foil stars, and a sheet of oak tag. With these items, students will create a replica of a spiral galaxy. Use the illustration on page 14 as a pattern for the shape of the center and the arms of the galaxy. Students will need to paint the center yellow and the arms blue, and attach sequins and foil stars to represent the stars and planets in the galaxy. Arms will need to be glued to the back of the yellow center. The brad should be put through the center of the yellow circle. These spiral galaxies could be incorporated into the mural in the following activity.

9. Read the Hirsts' *My Place in Space* and have the students write their own galactic addresses. Begin with each student's home address, then add their planet, their solar system, their galaxy, and their universe. Explain to students that they will now create a wall mural depicting their addresses. Cover a wall with white butcher paper. In the center of the paper, paste a map of your community. Let each student put a sticker on the exact location of her or his home. Next, divide students into groups and let the first group create a representation of the earth for the mural. The next group will illustrate the solar system, and so on. As they illustrate their assigned areas, have groups also add several important facts about their addition to the mural. Have each group share their facts with the class when the mural is completed.

10. Before sharing Lauber's *How We Learned the Earth Is Round*, ask students to volunteer to bring one ball, one empty tin can, and one paper plate from home. You will need to have three yardsticks, tape, string, and a flashlight on hand. After the reading, ask students to work in three groups, each using one of the three items students brought from home, to recreate the experiments on pages 16 and 17 of Lauber's book. Have each group perform their experiment for the entire class and discuss the results.

11. Read Cherry's *The Armadillo from Amarillo*. Show students a map of the school, the neighborhood, the city, the state, the United States, the world, and the solar system. Find the school's location on each map. Now make a class video of the the school's place in the universe. Begin with a shot of the students standing at the front door of the school. End with students looking at a globe with black paper (the night sky) behind it.

Allow students to think of creative strategies to depict all other shots. Share the class video with other classes.

12. Read Robinson's *Space Probes to the Planets* and then divide the class into teams of nine students. Allow each team member to select the planet they wish to illustrate and report on. Supply each team with black construction paper, heavy white paper, paints, brushes, and paste. Students should cut the shape of their planet out of the white paper and paint their planet in a realistic manner. Have Robinson's book available as a reference tool. Mount each planet on a piece of large black paper. Explain to students that they will be presenting the planets in the order they occur naturally, starting from the sun and moving outward to Pluto. Students will need to stand in this order in front of the class holding their planet picture. They will need to give two facts about their planet.

13. After reading, Kitamura's *UFO Diary*, allow students to choose a planet they would like to visit. Instruct students to make a diary telling and illustrating what they might see on their planet. They will need to go to the media center to find information on the planet they chose to visit. After students have completed their diaries, have the diaries available for other students to read.

FOLLOW-UP ACTIVITIES FOR INDIVIDUALS AND SMALL GROUPS

1. Read page 12 of Herbert's *Mr. Wizard's Supermarket Science*. Try this activity at home. Then bring materials for the activity to school and demonstrate how to make a constellation in your room.

2. Locate a copy of Stott's *Night Sky* and read pages 8 and 9. Prepare a night sky notebook and do the flashlight activity to view the night sky. Keep your notebook for documentation and share your findings with your classmates.

3. Read pages 12 and 13 of Stott's *Night Sky* and follow the instructions on doing the light experiment. Demonstrate the experiment for your classmates and explain how it relates to the stars.

4. Read pages 36 and 37 of Stott's *Night Sky* and follow the directions to make your own crater similar to the craters on Mercury. Share your crater with your class.

5. Read pages 40 and 41 of Stott's *Night Sky* and follow the directions on how to recreate the phases of the moon at your home. After you have practiced, demonstrate the recreation to your class and explain how it relates to the phases of the moon.

6. Read pages 130 and 131 of Drake and Love's *The Kid's Summer Handbook*. Borrow this book to take home and follow the directions on page 131 to help you find constellations. Repeat this activity for three nights. Each night, record which constellations you found. Draw a picture of those constellations and share the picture with your teacher.

7. Read pages 90 through 92 of Irvine's *Build It with Boxes*. Gather the materials and follow the directions to make the shadow theater. When the theater is completed, put on a simple performance for classmates.

■

ENERGY AND MOTION

STUDENT OBJECTIVES

1. Determine the reaction of magnets to various substances.
2. List simple machines that make work easier.
3. Identify different kinds of energy and their properties.

RECOMMENDED READINGS

Ardley, Neil. *The Science Book of Sound*. Photography by Dave King. Harcourt Brace Jovanovich, 1991. (Objective 3)
This book of simple experiments relates results with happenings in nature.

Berger, Melvin. *Switch On, Switch Off*. Illustrated by Carolyn Croll. Thomas Y. Crowell, 1989. (Objective 3)
This information book describes the principles basic to an understanding of electricity.

Branley, Franklyn M. *Air Is All Around You*. Illustrated by Holly Keller. HarperCollins, 1986. (Objective 3)
This information book describes the importance and power of air.

————. *Gravity Is a Mystery*. Illustrated by Don Madden. Thomas Y. Crowell, 1986. (Objective 3)
This information book describes the principle of gravity.

Browne, Eileen. *No Problem*. Illustrated by David Parkins. Candlewick Press, 1993. (Objectives 2 & 3)
Mouse and friends build a variety of interesting machines before reading the instructions.

Hines, Gary. *Flying Firefighters.* Illustrations by Anna Grossnickle Hines. Clarion, 1993. (Objective 2)
Hines describes the various tools needed to fight a forest fire.

Horvatic, Ann. *Simple Machines.* Photographs by Stephen Bruner. E.P. Dutton, 1989. (Objective 2)
Black-and-white photographs help students understand what simple machines are and how they work.

Marston, Hope Irvin. *Big Rigs.* Cobblehill, 1993. (Objective 2)
Using simple text and wonderful photographs, this book describes a variety of trucks and their uses.

Orii, Eiji, and Orii, Masako. *Simple Science Experiments with Light.* Illustrations by Kimimaro Yoshida. Gareth Stevens Children's Books, 1989. (Objective 3)
This information book contains simple experiments using light that students can replicate at home or school.

————. *Simple Science Experiments with Marbles.* Illustrated by Kaoru Fujishima. Gareth Stevens Children's Books, 1989. (Objective 3)
This information book offers easy-to-follow investigations about motion using only marbles and coins.

————. *Simple Science Experiments with Ping-Pong Balls.* Illustrated by Kimimaro Yoshida. Gareth Stevens Children's Books, 1989. (Objective 3)
A variety of investigations using household objects demonstrate the power of air.

————. *Simple Science Experiments with Starting and Stopping.* Illustrated by Kaoru Fujishima. Gareth Stevens Children's Books, 1989. (Objective 3)
This information book presents easy-to-follow experiments that investigate motion.

————. *Simple Science Experiments with Water.* Illustrated by Kaoru Fujishima. Gareth Stevens Children's Books, 1989. (Objective 3)
This information book highlights simple investigations that explore the properties of water.

Roll Along: Poems on Wheels. Poems selected by Myra Cohn Livingston. Macmillan, 1993. (Objective 2)
This is a collection of poems about many transportation vehicles with wheels.

Wade, Alan. *I'm Flying!* Illustrated by Petra Mathers. Alfred A. Knopf, 1990. (Objectives 2 & 3)
A young boy launches a variety of his most disliked objects in creative ways.

Walpole, Brenda. *175 Science Experiments to Amuse and Amaze Your Friends: Experiments! Tricks! Things to Make!* Illustrated by Kuo Kang Chen and Peter Bull. Random House, 1988. (Objectives 1, 2, & 3)
This experiment book covers a wide variety of topics with easy-to-follow directions and valuable illustrations.

————. *Water.* Photographs by Ed Barber. Garrett Educational Corporation, 1990. (Objective 3)
This information book describes the power of water in our everyday lives and provides easy-to-follow water experiments.

GROUP INTRODUCTORY ACTIVITY

Preparing for the Activity: Locate a copy of Browne's *No Problem* and gather a variety of building toys, such as Legos and Tinker Toys. Have available for each student a clean butter tub or plastic bucket. Attach a note to each tub or bucket similar to the one in Browne's book:

> To (student's name):
> Put together the things you see.
> Then climb aboard and visit me!
> Love from Your Teacher.

In each bucket, place duplicate sets of building toys. Have these materials on each student's desk when they arrive in the morning or after recess. The teacher will also need to build a machine using the same set of materials that each student is supplied. The teacher needs to write down the directions for building the machine and needs to place the machine somewhere where students will not see it.
Focus: Tell students they will find a bucket and a note on their desk and that they will need to pretend they are a small mouse when they read their note. Then allow students time to build and name their machine.
Objective: To satisfy the objectives of recognizing machines that make life easier and identifying different energy sources, bring the students together in a group and allow each child to show her or his invention and tell its name. Ask students to describe:

• What will make their machine go.

• How their machine travels.

• Whether it could hold more than one mouse.

• How fast their machine travels.

• What is special about their machine.

Then share Browne's book.

Extending Activity: After sharing, have students go back to their desks with their machines. Explain to students that there was another machine that could be built using the same materials they used for their machines. As the teacher reads the instructions for building that particular machine, have students build the machine following the directions. Ask the same questions about this machine and have students give the machine a name. Students could select their favorite machine from among all the machines made by the class. The teacher could help that student write directions for making her or his machine. Finally, each child could build the favorite machine.

FOLLOW-UP ACTIVITIES FOR
TEACHER AND STUDENTS TO SHARE

1. Introduce the Oriis' *Simple Science Experiments with Light* by asking if students have ever wondered how light affects the things they see. Explain that this book contains experiments about light that can be done at school or at home with an adult. Read aloud the directions for the experiments on pages 22 through 27. Ask for students to gather around a table while the teacher demonstrates the experiments. Now let several children perform the experiments. Explain to the students that the book is available for them to take home.

2. Introduce the Oriis' *Simple Science Experiments with Water* by asking students if they know why some things float and others sink. Ask students to name things that sink and float. Write their responses on the board. Read pages 3 and 4 to students and ask them to make a hypothesis about which fruits and vegetables will sink and which will float. Explain to students that a hypothesis is telling what you think might possibly happen as an end result. Perform the experiment at a demonstration table. Divide students into six to eight small groups and allow each group to demonstrate one of the other experiments in this book. Give groups time to practice their demonstrations. Each group should perform its experiment for the class. Remind groups to ask the class to make a hypothesis about the investigation before the demonstration begins. After the demonstration, compare the results with the students' hypothesis.

3. Introduce Walpole's *Water* by asking students to list how they use water in their everyday lives. Write these responses on the board. Next read Walpole's book over several days. Allow small groups of students to perform the experiments on pages 11, 12, and 15. After the group has performed the experiment, invite the group members to demonstrate the investigation for the whole class. Remind groups to ask the class to make a hypothesis about the experiment before the demonstration begins.

After the demonstration, compare the results with the students' hypothesis.

4. Introduce the Oriis' *Simple Science Experiments with Starting and Stopping* by asking students if they ever wondered what makes things start and stop. Explain that this book contains experiments explaining motion. Read page 3 and ask students to gather around a table where the teacher has gathered five wooden blocks and a wooden hammer. Next, demonstrate the experiments on pages 3 through 6. As you read the experiments, pause and let students try to answer the questions posed by the authors. Divide students into groups and supply each group with the materials necessary to demonstrate one of the investigations on pages 7 through 16. Have each group perform and explain their experiment to the class.

5. Introduce the Oriis' *Simple Science Experiments with Marbles* by asking students if they ever wondered what they could learn about movement from marbles. Explain that this book contains experiments using marbles that can be done at home or school with an adult. Read page 3 and ask students to gather around a table where the teacher has prepared a track according to the directions on page 3. Demonstrate the experiment on page 3 for students. Next, read page 5 and invite students to make guesses about the outcomes of this activity. Ask a student to assist as the teacher follows the directions on page 5. Read students the information on page 6 and ask if that explanation matches what they observed. Next, select students to demonstrate the investigations on pages 7 through 14. Discuss these experiments as they are performed. Explain to students that all of the materials necessary to perform the remaining investigations will remain on the table for them to try.

6. Introduce the Oriis' *Simple Science Experiments with Ping-Pong Balls* by asking students if they ever wanted to know more about the power of air. Explain that this book contains experiments with air. Read page 3 and ask students to gather around a table where the teacher has placed a glass, a candle, and a cloth. Demonstrate the experiment on page 3. Read page 4 and ask if that explanation matches what they observed. Now divide students into small groups. Supply each group with the materials necessary to demonstrate one of the investigations on pages 14 through 17 and 20 through 27. Have each group perform and explain their experiment to the class. To conclude this project, share Branley's *Air Is All Around You* with students. As a class, perform the experiments on pages 9 through 17, comparing this activity with the experiments from Orii's book. Ask students to find similarities between the two books.

7. Introduce Ardley's *The Science Book of Sound* by reading pages 6 and 7. Read and do the experiments on pages 12 through 15. Be sure to read the information on page 13 that relates traveling sound waves to sliding snow. Also be sure to highlight the information that relates paper noisemakers to thunderclaps.

8. Before sharing Marston's *Big Rigs*, have students brainstorm all the things that big trucks are used for. Make a list of their ideas on the chalkboard and then share Marston's book with students. After sharing, provide each student with a cut out of a big truck. Have the students label the truck with the appropriate parts. Each cut out might be a little different so as to include a variety of trucks mentioned in the book.

9. Explain to students that Horvatic's *Simple Machines* will teach them about five kinds of simple machines. Write the names of the simple machines on small strips of paper and have each student draw a slip of paper out of a hat. Explain to students they will need to listen carefully for information on their simple machine. Then share Horvatic's book with the class. After reading, have students find a few simple machines of their kind in the school or on the playground. Students will work with other students who have the same simple machine listed on their slip of paper. Allow students time to share their information with the class. Also have students keep a list of every machine that they use over a two-day period. Have students share their lists with the class at the end of the two-day period.

10. Prior to this activity, gather the necessary supplies to do the experiments listed on pages 92 and 93 of Walpole's *175 Science Experiments to Amuse and Amaze Your Friends: Experiments! Tricks! Things to Make!* Read Branley's *Gravity Is a Mystery* to students and then read pages 92 and 93 of Walpole's book. Ask three small groups of students to perform one of the three experiments on these pages. Have groups demonstrate their experiment to the class and have the class discuss the results of the experiments.

11. Share Wade's *I'm Flying!* with students. Use the experiment on page 59 of Walpole's *175 Science Experiments to Amuse and Amaze Your Friends: Experiments! Tricks! Things to Make!* to show students how to make a hot air balloon. Allow each student to make a balloon as described on this page. The teacher can then launch the balloons using the hair dryer method described in Walpole's book.

12. Prior to sharing Hines' *Flying Firefighters* with students, ask them to listen for all the different kinds of tools used to fight a forest fire. After sharing Hines' book, write the students' list of tools on the chalkboard. After the list is complete, divide it into two smaller lists: one of human-powered

tools and one of tools powered by a different form of energy. Have students choose a different profession, maybe a doctor, nurse, pilot, police officer, secretary, garbage collector, custodian, weathercaster, grocery store stocker, or teacher. Then have the students make a list of all the tools used by the people in the profession they chose. Have students share their information with a partner.

13. Prior to this activity, gather materials to make electricity as outlined in Berger's *Switch On, Switch Off*. Ask students to name the types of energy used in the school and in their homes. Record their responses on the board. Ask students if they know how electricity is made. Explain that the class will make electricity. Read Berger's book to students. Demonstrate how to make electricity as outlined on pages 10 through 13.

FOLLOW-UP ACTIVITIES FOR
INDIVIDUALS AND SMALL GROUPS

1. Read the experiment on page 8 of Ardley's *The Science Book of Sound*. Practice this experiment and then demonstrate it for your classmates. Be sure to read the information on sound vibration on page 9. You might also wish to make the rubber guitar on pages 24 and 25.

2. Reread Marston's *Big Rigs* and make a replica of a big rig using household items such as toilet paper rolls, cereal boxes, and a variety of lids. "Load" your big rig with cargo and display it in the classroom.

3. Reread Horvatic's *Simple Machines*. Go home and find an example of one of the five simple machines mentioned in the book. Bring it to school and share it with classmates.

4. Read page 63 in Walpole's *175 Science Experiments to Amuse and Amaze Your Friends: Experiments! Tricks! Things to Make!* Practice the experiment that demonstrates the power of air and show the experiment to your class.

5. You may want to ask for the help of several friends for this project. Reread Branley's *Gravity Is a Mystery*. Next, read page 94 in Walpole's *175 Science Experiments to Amuse and Amaze Your Friends: Experiments! Tricks! Things to Make!* Practice the experiment that demonstrates gravity and weight and show the experiment to your class.

6. Read several of the poems in *Roll Along: Poems on Wheels*. Choose your favorite, memorize it, and recite it for the class. Also draw a picture to illustrate your poem.

■

Ecology

STUDENT OBJECTIVES

1. Name and describe several types of pollution, such as noise, water, air, and land.
2. Describe several methods of pollution control.
3. Describe the environment in which dinosaurs lived.
4. Name and give some examples of the Earth's fragile environments.

RECOMMENDED READINGS

Accorsi, William. *Rachel Carson*. Holiday House, 1993. (Objectives 1 & 2)
This simple biography of environmentalist Rachel Carson beautifully illustrates the meaning of her life.

The Big Book for Our Planet. Written by Aliki, et al. Illustrated by Aliki, et al. Dutton Children's Books, 1993. (Objectives 1 & 2)
A selection of beautiful and moving short stories, illustrations, and poems that focus on our planet, Earth.

Brandenberg, Aliki. *Fossils Tell of Long Ago*. Thomas Y. Crowell, 1990. (Objective 3)
Aliki explains how fossils develop and why they are important today.

Brown, Ruth. *The World That Jack Built*. Dutton Children's Books, 1991. (Objectives 1 & 2)
Brown's beautiful illustrations coupled with a reworded traditional rhyme paint a vivid picture of environmental pollution.

Bunting, Eve. *Someday a Tree*. Illustrated by Ronald Himler. Clarion, 1993. (Objectives 1 & 2)
Alice is sad about the needless death of her favorite tree until she finds a hopeful solution.

Cherry, Lynne. *The Great Kapok Tree: A Tale of the Amazon Rain Forest*. Harcourt Brace Jovanovich, 1990. (Objectives 1, 2, & 4)
Gorgeous illustrations help to tell the story of a young man's decision not to cut down a tree in the rain forest.

Cole, Joanna. *The Magic School Bus at the Waterworks*. Illustrated by Bruce Degen. Scholastic, 1986. (Objectives 1 & 2)
Ms. Frizzle takes students on a tour of the waterworks.

Drake, Jane, and Love, Ann. *The Kid's Summer Handbook*. Illustrated by Heather Collins. Ticknor & Fields, 1994. (Objectives 1, 2, & 3)
This activity guide provides wonderful ideas for children to try.

Dunphy, Madeleine. *Here Is the Tropical Rain Forest*. Illustrated by Michael Rothman. Hyperion Books for Children, 1994 (Objective 4)
Clever lyrics show the unique relationship between plants and animals in the rain forest.

Elkington, John; Hailes, Julia; Merkower, Joel; and Hill, Douglas. *Going Green: A Kid's Handbook to Saving the Planet*. Illustrated by Tony Ross. Puffin Books, 1990. (Objectives 1 & 2)
This excellent resource and project guide for older elementary students provides practical suggestions for saving the planet.

Foster, Joanna. *Cartons, Cans and Orange Peels: Where Does Your Garbage Go?* Clarion Books, 1991. (Objective 2)
Foster presents a variety of ways to get rid of or take care of garbage.

Gibbons, Gail. *Recycle! A Handbook for Kids*. Little, Brown and Company, 1992. (Objective 2)
Interesting, fun illustrations and simple text describe recycling, its effects, and ways to recycle.

Gutnik, Martin J. *Experiments That Explore Recycling*. Illustrated by Sharon Lane Holm. Millbrook Press, 1992. (Objective 2)
Gutnik provides a variety of activities that examine recycling.

Hirschi, Ron. *Where Are My Prairie Dogs and Black-Footed Ferrets?* Photographs by Erwin and Peggy Bauer and others. Bantam Books, 1992. (Objectives 1, 2, & 4)
Using photographs and text, Hirschi describes the plight of grasslands and prairies.

Irvine, Joan. *Build It with Boxes*. Illustrated by Linda Hendry. Morrow Junior Books, 1993. (Objective 3)
Irvine provides many fun projects to make with boxes.

Koch, Michelle. *World Water Watch*. Greenwillow Books, 1993. (Objective 1)
Koch's simple text tells what precautions are being made to protect six different animals from extinction.

Lauber, Patricia. *Living with Dinosaurs.* Illustrated by Douglas Henderson. Bradbury, 1991. (Objective 3)
This information book provides an excellent description of the world in which dinosaurs lived and their role in the development of fossil fuels.

―――. *The News About Dinosaurs.* Bradbury Press, 1989. (Objective 3)
Lauber provides new ways of thinking about dinosaurs.

Leedy, Loreen. *The Great Trash Bash.* Holiday House, 1991. (Objective 2)
The residents of Beaston begin to realize the need to improve their environment.

Most, Bernard. *Where to Look for a Dinosaur.* Harcourt Brace Jovanovich, 1993. (Objective 3)
Most's cleverly illustrated book presents many types of dinosaurs, as well as the dinosaurs' relationship to fossil fuel and to the environment.

Nolan, Dennis. *Dinosaur Dream.* Macmillan, 1990. (Objective 3)
Wilbur's fantasy takes him back to the time of dinosaurs.

Walpole, Brenda. *175 Science Experiments to Amuse and Amaze Your Friends: Experiments! Tricks! Things to Make!* Illustrated by Kuo Kang Chen and Peter Bull. Random House, 1988. (Objectives 1 & 2)
This experiment book covers a wide variety of topics by using easy-to-follow directions and valuable illustrations.

Yolen, Jane. *Welcome to the Greenhouse.* Illustrated by Laura Regan. G.P. Putnam's Sons, 1993. (Objectives 1, 2, & 4)
Beautiful text and lush illustrations depict life in the rain forest.

GROUP INTRODUCTORY ACTIVITY

Preparing for the Activity: Secure a copy of each of the following books: Yolen's *Welcome to the Greenhouse,* Cherry's *The Great Kapok Tree: A Tale of the Amazon Rain Forest,* and Hirschi's *Where Are My Prairie Dogs and Black-Footed Ferrets?* Hang three mural-sized sheets of kraft paper around the classroom. Obtain construction paper, fabric scraps, twine, string, yarn, dried grasses, colored chalk, crayons, colored pencils, and wrapping paper.
Focus: Begin by reading Yolen's book. On different days, share Cherry's and Hirschi's books with the class. After each reading, discuss the environmental problems related to each habitat, including prairies, rain forests, and grasslands. Ask students to think about environmental problems surrounding their favorite outdoor play area, a local park, or the school playground. Explain to students that they will select one of three habitats to recreate in mural form in the classroom. Allow students to choose the habitat in which they wish to

work. Divide students into groups organized by habitat. Have each group brainstorm ideas for their mural. Have groups create a rough draft of their mural ideas that defines each member's responsibilities for the creation of the mural and depicts the basic design of the mural.

Objective: To satisfy the objectives of being aware of the categories of pollution and methods of pollution control, ask students to add two final segments to their murals. One segment should depict the dangers that threaten their habitat and one segment should illustrate solutions for the environmental dangers violating their habitat.

Extending Activity: Supply students with materials to create their murals. Give students ample time to work on this project. When the murals are completed, invite other classes to view the murals. Have students prepare a brief narrative to accompany these viewings. This narrative could be in written or oral form or both.

FOLLOW-UP ACTIVITIES FOR
TEACHER AND STUDENTS TO SHARE

1. After reading Brown's *The World That Jack Built*, ask students to generate a list of types of pollution shown in this book (air, water, land). Ask them to think of other types of pollution to add to the list. Finally, ask them how people in their own community (the school) contribute to pollution problems. Have each student select one type of pollution and research ways to prevent it. Each student should then develop a poster showing one way to prevent the type of pollution he or she researched. Display the posters in a school hallway.

2. Read Gibbons' *Recycle!: A Handbook for Kids* and ask the class to generate a list of ways they could put recycling to work at school. List their ideas on the board. Most students will list paper recycling, aluminum can recycling, and newspaper recycling. Begin providing bins for newspapers, paper, and aluminum cans in the school. Have students collect the recyclable trash and take it to a recycling center. Have students select ways to use their refunds to buy new trash cans or pollution recycling bins or something related to fighting pollution.

3. Before reading Leedy's *The Great Trash Bash*, take a walk around the school. Ask students to look for any areas around the school that need attention or any areas where they see an environmental problem. This walk could take place both inside and outside of the school. Upon returning to class, help students list any problem areas they encountered. Ask students to be on the lookout for environmental problem areas in their community. Suggest that students keep a journal over the weekend to document environmental problem areas around their neighborhoods

and homes. The following Monday, have students share their findings. Have pairs of students create classified ads inviting community members to participate in a cleaner environment. Students should use original ideas and ideas from the back of Leedy's book to develop their ads. A sample ad might be:

WANTED: CLEANER ROADSIDES

Stop before you throw litter out of your car!

Keep a sack for trash in your car.

(Students' first names and ages)

Ask the local newspaper to run the students' classified ads as a community environmental awareness project. If the local newspaper cannot absorb the cost of running such an ad, a local bank, school business partner, or vendor might be willing to incur the cost.

4. Read Most's *Where to Look for a Dinosaur* and discuss what happened to dinosaurs and other animals in danger of extinction. Have pairs of students select an endangered species to research, using encyclopedias, nature books, and other library resources to find the following details about their endangered species:

- Name of the endangered species
- A description of the animal
- Location (Where can the animal be found?)
- What does the animal need to survive?
- Why is it endangered?
- What measures are being taken to prevent its extinction?
- Where would a person write or call if interested in helping save the animal?

After students gather their data, ask them to write a two-paragraph newspaper article to be included in a class newspaper on endangered species. Have several students act as coeditors to gather articles and compile them into your school's *Eco Times*. Use a simple children's writing or publishing software program to produce a finished project. The teacher may want to limit the amount of data gathered by younger students.

5. Before sharing Koch's *World Water Watch*, divide students into six groups and provide each group of students with big cut outs of the following animals: sea otter, sea turtle, penguin, fur seal, polar bear, and humpback whale. After reading Koch's book, have students answer the following questions and record their answers on the large cut outs of their animals:

- What problem is their specific animal having?
- Where in the world is their animal located?

Have students memorize the poem at beginning of book and allow them
to do a presentation for other classes. Their presentation should include
all the students reciting the poem. Next, each group should share information about their animal while holding up their animal cut out. At the
end of the presentation, have students recite the poem once again, but
this time allow the audience to participate.

6. Share several chapters of Foster's *Cartons, Cans and Orange Peels: Where
    Does Your Garbage Go?* that relate to home garbage. Give each student
    eight grocery sacks and ask them to label the sacks as follows:

    Label two sacks PAPER
    Label two sacks PLASTIC
    Label two sacks GLASS
    Label two sacks METAL

Ask students to keep a daily log of their trash at home for two days. Have
students use their labelled sacks to sort the trash at their home. Ask
them to record how many glass items, paper items, metal items, and plastic items were thrown away. After two days, have each student graph her
or his data to compare how much of each type of trash was thrown away
each day. A simple bar graph format can be used. Have students give
theories about why there was more trash one day than another. Graph
the results of the entire class. Ask students if they see any similarities in
the data and if any conclusions can be drawn from these findings.

7. Share Aliki's *Fossils Tell of Long Ago* with students. Using clay, make im-
    pressions of students' thumbs as explained by Aliki. Each student should
    have his or her own clay mold. Explain to students that they will be
    creating a class time capsule to be opened during their last year in that
    school building. Their time capsule should include their "fossil" thumb
    prints and other information that will identify the time period. This might
    include newspapers, magazines, photographs, school newsletters, and year-
    books. The class should record the location and date for the time capsule
    to be opened and submit this information to the school principal. An
    opening ceremony should be planned for the future.

8. Read Dunphy's *Here Is the Tropical Rain Forest*. Discuss the special rela-
    tionship between the plants and the animals of the rain forest. Stress
    how these plants and animals depend on one another. Ask students to
    create a mural depicting the lyrics from Dunphy's book. For example, the
    first panel of the mural should show a picture of a lush rain forest. The
    next panel would depict the frog under the bromeliad, the next would
    show the bromeliad in the tree, and so on. Provide students with paints,
    markers, fabric scraps, construction paper, tissue paper, and other collage
    materials to use for their mural.

9. Share Lauber's *Living with Dinosaurs* with students. Read several sections every day over a one-week period. End with the last chapter on fossils. Have students work together to make a mural depicting how fossils are made. Provide students with big kraft paper, colored chalk, and black markers for the mural. Use the illustrations on page 42 and 43 as a model. When the mural is complete, have students invite other classes to see their creation.

10. Read Babbitt's "The Last Days of the Giddywit" in *The Big Book for Our Planet* and lead a class discussion, using the following questions as a beginning point:

   - Do you know any people like those of the Giddywit tribe?
   - How were the Oogites different?
   - Which tribe's ideas do you like best?
   - How does our society deal with the problem of trash?

11. Read Conrad's "The Earth Game" in *The Big Book for Our Planet*. This is a perfect and very effective story to act out. Give each student an index card with his or her part printed on it. Each student part will be one of the quotes from the children doing the activity in the story. Thus, some children will have lines stating the pollution problem on our planet and other students will have lines that present solutions to our pollution problems. Next, have students connect themselves with a ball of twine as indicated in the story. As each student is connected, have them read or say their part. After practice, perform this play for other students and parents.

12. Read Bunting's *Someday a Tree* and lead a class discussion using the following questions:

   - What might have poisoned the oak tree?
   - Can you name other things on our planet that are being poisoned?
   - What environmental efforts do you know of that are aimed at helping clean up poisoned areas?
   - What poisonous things do you or your family get rid of? (pool water, paint, detergent water)

   Invite a local sanitation specialist to tell students how to dispose of possible poisons. Ask students to share this information with their parents.

13. Read Cole's *The Magic School Bus at the Waterworks* and then take students to a nearby puddle, pond, lake, or stream and collect a jar full of muddy water. Follow the directions on page 43 of Walpole's *175 Science Experiments to Amuse and Amaze Your Friends: Experiments! Tricks! Things*

to Make! to create a class water filter. Warn the children not to drink this water. The class might also visit a local waterworks plant.

14. Share Accorsi's *Rachel Carson* and ask students the following questions:

    • What were the most important things to Rachel?
    • What was Rachel's main goal?
    • Did she succeed?
    • Why do you think people listened to her?
    • Why was this book written about her?
    • Is what she believed still important to us today?

    Take time to discuss students' answers.

15. Share Nolan's *Dinosaur Dream* with students. Discuss Wilbur's adventures during his visit to the Jurassic period. Ask students to choose a dinosaur that they are interested in learning more about. Tell students they will be pretending to be that dinosaur and that their problem is a little different than the problem Wilbur had. Their dinosaur will be living in today's world. Explain to students that they will be keeping a diary for a day as the dinosaur they have chosen. Remind students that they will need an entry for each hour of the day and ask them to think about what problems the dinosaur might encounter.

16. Read pages 58 through 61 of Gutnik's *Experiments That Explore Recycling* to students. Follow the directions to make the paper on pages 60 and 61. The teacher or a parent volunteer will need to do the ironing for this project. It would also be fun for students to add food coloring to change the color of their paper. Students can use their paper to make collages; simply have them tear the edges of the paper instead of cutting. Display the collages in the classroom or hallway.

FOLLOW-UP ACTIVITIES FOR
INDIVIDUALS AND SMALL GROUPS

1. Read pages 194 and 195 of Drake and Love's *The Kid's Summer Handbook*. Ask your teacher for fossils or bring them from home. Follow the directions on page 195 to prepare rubbings, embossings, and clay prints of fossils. Share the fossil and your finished work with other students.

2. Follow the directions on page 60 of Drake and Love's *The Kid's Summer Handbook* to learn how to build a mini composter at your home. You will need to keep a composter diary. Check the composter twice a week for six weeks and record your observations. At the end of the six-week period, share your diary with other students.

2. Read pages 41 through 45 in Elkington's *Going Green: A Kid's Handbook to Saving the Planet* about the waste of water in the bathroom. Make a chart on poster board using the parts of the chart on page 17 that are related to bathroom waste. Share your chart statistics and ways to save water in the bathroom with your classmates. Share your findings with your parents.

4. Read pages 20 through 26 of Elkington's *Going Green: A Kid's Handbook to Saving the Planet* to understand the problems of trash in our country. Collect recycled items from home that use the symbol found on page 25 or some other note about recycling. Prepare a display of these items to teach your classmates how to look at products to see if they are recycled.

5. This activity is for strong readers. Read Lauber's *The News About Dinosaurs* and then find several statements showing that scientists have revised their findings on dinosaur research. Write down the scientists' previous ideas and their current ideas and share them with a classmate.

6. Read pages 62 and 63 of Irvine's *Build It with Boxes*. Gather the materials needed and ask for a parent or teacher to help you make the triceratops costume. Bring the costume to school and try it on for your classmates.

■

NONPRINT SOURCES FOR GRADES 2-3

Prior to using any of these nonprint sources, read all of the accompanying documentation and preview the application. The literature accompanying many of these products suggests appropriate uses. Determine if the material is to be used by the entire class, by small groups of students, or by an individual student. After choosing the audience for the nonprint material selected, it will be necessary to teach students how to use the application.

LIFE SCIENCE—ANIMALS

Bugs. Reading Rainbow Series, GPN. VHS videocassette.
A variety of insect lives and habitats are studied and viewed.

Humphrey the Lost Whale: A True Story. Reading Rainbow Series, GPN. VHS videocassette.
This video chronicles the lives of humpback whales.

Odell Down Under. MECC. Mac or Windows versions.
Students explore animals, plants, and the food chain of the Great Barrier Reef.

Shark Alert. Philips Interactive Media, 1993. CD-I.
This interactive CD program allows students to choose from a variety of video clips, stories, facts, and games that teach about sharks.

A World of Animals. National Geographic Society, 1993. Mac CD-ROM.
This computer book provides students with an interactive approach to learning and recalling information about animals.

LIFE SCIENCE—PLANTS

Lunar Greenhouse. MECC, 1989. Apple II software.
This simulation requires students to find the optimum conditions for plant growth.

Odell Down Under. MECC. Mac or Windows versions.
Students explore animals, plants, and the food chain of the Great barrier reef.

A World of Plants. National Geographic Society, 1993. Mac CD-ROM.
This computer book provides students with an interactive approach to learning and recalling information about plants.

HUMAN BODY

Cavity Busters. MECC, 1991. Apple II software.
This simulation allows students to investigate variables that affect healthy teeth.

Germs Make Me Sick! Reading Rainbow Series, GPN. VHS videocassette.
This video allows students to explore how the human body copes with germs.

The Human Body. National Geographic Society, 1993. Mac CD-ROM.
This computer book provides students with an interactive approach to learning and recalling information about the human body.

Nutrition Nabber. MECC. Apple II software.
This simulation requires students to identify nutritious foods.

EARTH SCIENCE

Our Earth. National Geographic Society, 1993. Mac CD-ROM.
This computer book provides students with an interactive approach to learning and recalling information about the Earth.

SPACE

Rocket Factory. MECC. Apple II and MS-DOS software.
This simulation game permits students to build and launch a rocket while investigating force, motion, and space travel.

ENERGY AND MOTION

Electrifying Adventures. MECC. Apple II and MS-DOS software.
This simulation game permits students to explore electricity.

Miner's Cave. MECC, 1988. Apple II and MS-DOS software.
This simulation game permits students to explore the uses of simple machines and force.

Mystery Matter. MECC, 1988. Apple II and MS-DOS software.
This simulation game permits students to explore matter and energy, including electricity, water, and magnetism.

Pizza to Go. MECC. Apple II software.
This simulation game permits students to explore the uses of simple machines and force.

Rocket Factory. MECC. Apple II and MS-DOS software.
This simulation game permits students to build and launch a rocket while investigating force, motion, and space travel.

Simple Machines: An Introduction to the Physical Sciences for Children Ages 8–14. Science for Kids. CD-ROM for Mac and Windows versions.
This CD-ROM program allows students to explore the importance of the six simple machines throughout history.

ECOLOGY

Choices, Choices: Kids and the Environment. Tom Snyder Productions. Mac software.
This simulation teaches students about and discusses environmental problems and solutions.

Cleanwater Detectives. MECC. Apple II software.
This simulation allows students to investigate water pollution.

Digging Up Dinosaurs. Reading Rainbow Series, GPN. VHS videocassette.
This video provides students with information on the life and the death of dinosaurs.

Eco-Saurus. Davidson & Associates, Inc. 1991. MS-DOS software.
This ecology awareness program introduces young students to the basic ecology and conservation concepts.

Jack, the Seal and the Sea. Reading Rainbow Series, GPN, 1990. VHS videocassette.
Students gain insight into the problems of sea pollution.

Microsoft Dinosaurs. Microsoft Corp. MS-DOS or Windows CD-ROM.
Students explore the lives of dinosaurs through pictures, tours, and written text.

CHAPTER
3

o x x x x « ◊ ◊

Fourth Grade/Fifth Grade

■

LIFE SCIENCE—ANIMALS

STUDENT OBJECTIVES

1. Observe and describe how the structure and function of animals enable them to compete and survive in a community.
2. Describe the life cycles of animals.
3. Classify animals into vertebrates and invertebrates.

RECOMMENDED READINGS

Arnold, Caroline. *On the Brink of Extinction: The California Condor.* Photographs by Michael Wallace. Harcourt Brace Jovanovich, 1993. (Objective 1)
Beautiful photographs and text describe human attempts to save the condors.

Arnosky, Jim. *Crinkleroot's Book of Animal Tracking.* Bradbury Press, 1989. (Objective 1)
Arnosky's fun character explains what can be learned from animal tracks.

Bernhard, Emery. *Ladybug.* Illustrated by Durga Bernhard. Holiday House, 1992, (Objective 2)
Lively illustrations and text describe historical and biological facts about
1When there is no auxiliary, we have to supply one.
ladybugs.

Brandenburg, Jim. *Sand and Fog: Adventures in Southern Africa.* Walker and Company, 1994. (Objectives 1 & 2)
Vivid photographs and text depict the endangered habitat of the Namibia desert and Etosha National Park.

Cerullo, Mary M. *Sharks: Challengers of the Deep*. Photographs by Jeffrey L. Rotman. Cobblehill, 1993. (Objectives 1, 2, & 3)
Rotman's photographs, coupled with Cerullo's informative text, provide an excellent book about sharks.

Cowcher, Helen. *Tigress*. Farrar, Straus and Giroux, 1991. (Objective 2)
Vivid illustrations and simple text describe the cycle of life that hinges on the tigress.

Dewey, Jennifer. *Animal Architecture*. Orchard, 1991. (Objective 1)
Beautiful pencil drawings and text provide information on where and how a variety of animals live.

Facklam, Margery. *The Big Bug Book*. Illustrated by Paul Facklam. Little, Brown and Company, 1994. (Objectives 1, 2, & 3)
This information book describes unusually large bugs and illustrates their actual sizes using common objects for comparison.

Goor, Ron, and Goor, Nancy. *Insect Metamorphosis*. Atheneum, 1990. (Objective 2)
Vivid photographs and text describe insect metamorphosis.

Knight, Linsay. *The Sierra Club Book of Small Mammals*. Sierra Club Books for Children, 1993. (Objectives 1, 2, & 3)
Using text, photographs, and drawings, this information book describes a wide variety of small mammals.

Lacey, Elizabeth A. *What's the Difference?: A Guide to Some Familiar Animal Look-Alikes*. Illustrated by Robert Shetterly. Clarion, 1993. (Objective 1)
Lacey explains the differences between animals that look similar, such as a rabbit and a hare.

Lauber, Patricia. *Alligators: A Success Story*. Illustrated by Lou Silva. Henry Holt and Company, Inc., 1993. (Objectives 1 & 2)
Using vivid photographs and drawings, Lauber describes the adaptibility of alligators.

Lindblad, Lisa. *The Serengeti Migration: Africa's Animals on the Move*. Photographs by Sven-Olof Lindblad. Hyperion Books for Children, 1994. (Objectives 1 & 2)
Vivid photographs and thorough text describe the yearly migration of animals to Serengeti National Park.

London, Jonathan. *Voices of the Wild*. Crown, 1993. (Objectives 1, 2, & 3)
London provides information on a variety of animals and their encounters with humans.

Machotka, Hana. *Breathtaking Noses.* Morrow, 1992. (Objective 1)
Machotka's wonderful photographs and simple text provide readers with information on a variety of animal noses.

————. *Terrific Tails.* Morrow, 1994. (Objective 1)
Machotka's wonderful photographs and simple text provide readers with information on a variety of animal tails.

Maestro, Betsy. *Take a Look at Snakes.* Illustrated by Giulio Maestro. Scholastic, Inc., 1992. (Objectives 1, 2, & 3)
Maestro's book describes characteristics, behaviors, and habitats of a variety of snakes.

McMillan, Bruce. *A Beach for the Birds.* Houghton Mifflin, 1993. (Objective 1)
Photographs and prose illustrate the beauty and the plight of the Least Terns.

Parker, Nancy Winslow. *Working Frog.* Greenwillow, 1992. (Objective 3)
Parker relates the story of a frog that lives in the reptile house at the Bronx Zoo from the frog's point of view.

Patent, Dorothy Hinshaw. *What Good Is a Tail?* Dutton's Children's Books, 1994. (Objective 1)
Beautiful photographs and text document the importance of animals' tails.

Roop, Peter, and Roop, Connie. *One Earth, A Multitude of Creatures.* Illustrated by Valerie A. Kells. Walker and Company, 1992. (Objective 3)
Using beautiful illustrations and prose, this book explores the ecosystem of the earth.

Rosen, Michael J. *All Eyes on the Pond.* Illustrated by Tom Leonard. Hyperion Books for Children, 1994. (Objective 1)
Rosen uses brief text to describe the eyes of a variety of creatures.

Snedden, Robert. *What Is a Bird?* Photographs by Oxford Scientific Films. Illustrated by Adrian Lascom. Sierra Club Books for Children, 1993. (Objectives 1, 2, & 3)
This animal information book uses beautiful photographs, drawings, and text to describe the habitat, feeding habits, defenses, and reproduction of birds.

————. *What Is a Fish?* Photographs by Oxford Scientific Films. Illustrated by Adrian Lascom. Sierra Club Books for Children, 1993. (Objectives 1, 2, & 3)
This animal information book uses beautiful photographs, drawings, and text to describe the habitat, feeding habits, defenses, and reproduction of fish.

————. *What Is an Insect?* Photographs by Oxford Scientific Films. Illustrated by Adrian Lascom. Sierra Club Books for Children, 1993. (Objectives 1, 2, & 3)
This animal information book uses beautiful photographs, drawings, and text to describe the habitat, feeding habits, defenses, and reproduction of insects.

Tomb, Howard. *MicroAliens: Dazzling Journeys with an Electron Microscope.* Photographs by Dennis Kunkel. Illustrated by Tracy Dockray. Farrar, Straus and Giroux, 1993. (Objectives 1, 2, & 3)
Fantastic photographs show the world through the eye of an electron microscope.

Yolen, Jane. *Bird Watch: A Book of Poetry.* Illustrated by Ted Lewin. Philomel, 1990. (Objective 1)
Birds are described beautifully through poetry and illustrations.

GROUP INTRODUCTORY ACTIVITY

Preparing for the Activity: Locate London's *Voices of the Wild.* Have the following materials available: several books that identify animal tracks, quick-drying plaster of Paris, water, and a shovel.

Focus: Before reading, tell students that they will be identifying the animal tracks on the last page of London's book. Also have students help locate the man in each picture. Share London's book with students.

Objective: To satisfy the first and second objectives on animals' survival characteristics and life cycles, have students research how the animals in the book use their feet and why the shape and structure of the feet are important. Also, have students explain what the foot function of this animal has to do with its life cycle.

Extending Activity: Find an area near your school where animal tracks can be found. These could be dog, cat, or wild animal tracks and could be found even on your playground. Using quick-drying plaster of Paris, make molds of the different tracks. Label and display the molds in the library or classroom. If no tracks are available near your school, have students create tracks in dirt or sand using those in London's book as models. Then they can make molds of their creations.

FOLLOW-UP ACTIVITIES FOR
TEACHER AND STUDENTS TO SHARE

1. As you read Bernhard's *Ladybug* to students, create a timeline or chart on the chalkboard showing the stages of growth of the ladybug. After reading the book, ask small groups of students to research the life cycles of

one of the following insects: butterflies, ants, bees, grasshoppers, crickets, wasps, fleas, mosquitoes, and roaches. Have each group create its own timeline or chart depicting the insect's life cycle. Provide students with markers, large chart paper, and a variety of scrap papers and materials, including fabric, wallpaper samples, string, candy wrappers, and yarn. Explain to students that their insects should be presented using collage.

2. Share Maestro's *Take a Look at Snakes* and have students select a type of snake. Then have each student create a classified ad to sell their type of snake. Each student will have to research the snake to make the ad unique. Ads should reflect the habitat, characteristics, and behavior of the snake and should include an illustration of the snake. An example to share with students might be:

> For Sale: Large, Reticulated Python
> Needs Extra Long Home!
> Needs Many Small Animals to Squeeze
> And Digest!

3. As you read Arnosky's *Crinkleroot's Book of Animal Tracking*, have students answer each animal question asked throughout the book. Using pages 9, 21, and 28 as examples, ask students to create their own animal questions. Have each student select and research the habitat of one animal. Have students use their findings to create an animal question, using animal tracks or written clues to answer their question.

4. Before reading Machotka's *Breathtaking Noses*, have students spend five minutes listing everything they know about an elephant's nose or a pig's nose. As you read, show students the pictures of noses. Have students guess to whom the noses belong and then read information on the nose. After the reading, have students research how a variety of animals use their mouths. Have each student choose one animal to research, and then have them draw a picture of the mouth and provide facts to go with their picture. Put all of the illustrations and written information into a book and share it with the class.

5. Share the Roops' *One Earth, A Multitude of Creatures* with students. Describe the difference between vertebrates and invertebrates. Go through the book a second time with students and have them identify which animals are vertebrates and which are invertebrates.

6. Read Dewey's *Animal Architecture* to students. Divide students into pairs and have each pair select an animal's home they would like to build. This project may take several class periods. Supply students with building materials such as string, twigs, leaves, shredded paper, dirt, water, glue, grass, pieces of fabric, and newspaper. Some of these items may be col-

lected on the school grounds and some may be brought from home. Display animal homes in a central location in the school.

7. Begin by reading pages 7 through 15 of Arnold's *On the Brink of Extinction: The California Condor* and then read McMillan's *A Beach for the Birds*. After these books are read, discuss how the birds have become endangered. Ask students how humans have helped and hurt this species. Then have students work in pairs to select an endangered species, explain why it is endangered, and what humans are doing to aid that species. Students will then create brochures that share the information they found. Display the brochures in your school library.

8. After reading Parker's *Working Frog*, have students write an autobiography of a zoo animal. This will require each student to research his or her zoo animal and the zoo conditions in which it lives. A trip to a local zoo prior to this activity would allow students to investigate their animal's behavior and habitat.

9. Before reading Machotka's *Terrific Tails*, have students spend five minutes listing everything they know about a peacock's tail or a monkey's tail. As you read, show students the pictures of tails and ask them to guess to whom the tails belong. After reading Machotka's book, have students research how a variety of animals use their feet, hoofs, and legs. Have each student choose one animal to find information on, and then have them draw a picture of the feet and legs and provide facts to go with their picture. Put all of the illustrations and written information into a book and share it with the class.

10. Share several of the bugs in Facklam's *The Big Bug Book*, asking each student to select one common bug to research. The students will make a book using Facklam's format, with each student responsible for an illustration of their bug in its actual size and compared in size to a common object. Students will also be responsible for a narrative page describing where the bug is found, what it eats, unusual facts about the bug, and its popularity or lack of popularity with humans.

11. Before sharing Rosen's *All Eyes on the Pond*, conduct a brief discussion with students about their eyes. This discussion might include eye color, eye parts, and how human eyes are used. Then begin sharing Rosen's book. As each page is read, have students discuss how that particular animal uses its eyes, how each eye is unique, and if those were our eyes, how would they be useful or how would they hinder our ability to function. Have each student choose an animal and research its eyes.

12. Prior to sharing Lindblad's *The Serengeti Migration: Africa's Animals on the Move* and Brandenburg's *Sand and Fog: Adventures in Southern Africa*,

assign pairs of students one of the following items to research: Wilde-beests, Nasera Rock, Olduvai Gorge, Serengeti National Park, Kopjes (Moru Kopjes), Hyrax, Hartebeests, Elands, Topis, Lynx, Kudus, Skeleton Coast, Sand Grouse, Etosha Pan, Etosha National Park, Namibia Desert, and Springboks. Ask students to determine what their item is, where their item is, and interesting facts about their item. Students should find a picture of their assigned item to share with the class and give a brief synopsis of their research. Read Lindblad's and Bradenburg's books and compare the facts in these books with the facts found by students.

13. Before reading Patent's *What Good Is a Tail?*, have students list how different animals use their tails for protection and other uses. For example, beavers use their tails as an alarm system and to help them build their homes. After reading Patent's book, add examples given in the book to the class list.

14. Read several sections of Knight's *The Sierra Club Book of Small Mammals* to students. Students might enjoy the chapters entitled "Anteater, Armadillos, and Sloths" and "Pangolins," or have the book available for students to browse through prior to this activity and let them suggest chapters they would like to hear. After sharing several chapters, have students brainstorm a list of large mammals. Write their responses on the board. Have each student select one mammal to research. Have the students prepare a one-page document that includes animal name, scientific name, physical description, habitat, location, survival techniques, and diet. Students should also include a drawing of their animal. Bind the documents into a classroom book of large mammals.

15. Locate copies of Snedden's *What Is a Bird?*, *What Is a Fish?*, and *What Is an Insect?* Read the beginning section of each book, entitled "What Is...?", to the class. Tell students that the following are some of the areas included in each book:

- *What Is a Bird?* includes sections on feathers, songs, beaks, and eggs.
- *What Is a Fish?* includes sections on fins, gills, and barbels.
- *What Is an Insect?* includes sections on wings, lenses, and antennae.

After providing students with this information, allow each student to choose one area that he or she would like to research. Allow time for students to share their information with the class and to compare their findings with the findings in the book.

FOLLOW-UP ACTIVITIES FOR
INDIVIDUALS AND SMALL GROUPS

1. Find a small group of people to help you with this project. Using Machotka's *Breathtaking Noses* and *Terrific Tails* as models, create a similar book about animals' eyes, mouths, hooves, or skins. Present the completed book to your class.

2. Reread the first few pages of Arnold's *On the Brink of Extinction: The California Condor.* Then complete the book and share several facts about condors that were not given in class previously.

3. Read Cowcher's *Tigress* and then make a drawing of the cycle of life depicted in this book. Use a circle as the format for this drawing. Share both the book and your drawing with classmates.

4. Using the maps on the beginning pages of Lindblad's *The Serengeti Migration: Africa's Animals on the Move,* draw a similar map for a different species. You might draw a migration map for whales, geese, or butterflies.

5. Read the Goors' *Insect Metamorphosis* and choose an animal, not named in the book, that is matched. Describe that animal's change from an egg to an adult and share your description with your class. You may need to use library resources for your research.

6. Read several of Yolen's bird poems in *Bird Watch: A Book of Poetry.* Using a handbook on birds, birdwatch in your backyard or local park. Make a list of the kinds of birds you see, and include the number of each kind that you observed. Share your experience and pictures of the birds with your classmates.

7. Before reading Cerullo's *Sharks: Challengers of the Deep,* take the quiz on page 1 of the book. Record your answers on a sheet of paper. Then read Cerullo's book. Now retake the quiz and check your answers using pages 53 and 54. Choose a friend and ask him or her some of the questions. If the friend seems interested, tell her or him about Cerullo's book.

8. Read Lauber's *Alligators: A Success Story.* Using Lauber's examples, draw a chart showing common alligators, crocodiles, and gavials. Also make a chart depicting how fast a male alligator grows. Choose several alligator facts to share with a classmate. Also share your drawings with classmates.

9. Read Lacey's *What's the Difference?: A Guide to Some Familiar Animal Look-Alikes.* Choose one pair of animals to study. Find magazine pictures of the animals you have chosen and put the pictures on posterboard. Write down a number of differences between the animals and share these differences with a classmate.

10. Read pages 10 through 43 of Tomb's *MicroAliens: Dazzling Journeys with an Electron Microscope*. Borrow a microscope from your teacher and use it to look at several dead insects. Compare the detail you can see with the detail in the book. Show other students your insects and the insects in Tomb's book.

■

LIFE SCIENCE—PLANTS

STUDENT OBJECTIVES

1. Identify characteristics of major groups of plants such as trees, flowers, and algae.
2. Collect and identify a variety of plants.
3. Identify several poisonous plants.
4. Describe the life cycle of plants.

RECOMMENDED READINGS

Appelbaum, Diana. *Giants in the Land*. Illustrated by Michael McCurdy. Houghton Mifflin, 1993. (Objective 4)
This moving historical account chronicles how humans altered the life cycles of the great giant pines of the United States.

Arnosky, Jim. *Crinkleroot's Guide to Knowing the Trees*. Bradbury Press, 1992. (Objectives 1 & 2)
Arnosky's Crinkleroot character provides information about varieties and parts of trees and leaves.

Bush, Barbara. *Desert Giant: The World of the Saguaro Cactus*. Little, Brown and Company, 1989. (Objectives 1 & 4)
Bush gives a thorough portrait of the life of the saguaro cactus.

————. *Tree of Life: The World of the African Baobab*. Little, Brown and Company, 1989. (Objectives 1 & 4)
This book depicts how the ancient baobab supports a variety of life forms.

Chesworth, Michael. *Archibald Frisby*. Farrar, Straus and Giroux, 1994. (Objectives 1 & 4)
The reader follows Archibald Frisby, a boy who loves science, through a variety of adventures.

Creasy, Rosalind. *Blue Potatoes, Orange Tomatoes: How to Grow a Rainbow Garden*. Illustrated by Ruth Heller. Sierra Club Books for Children, 1994. (Objectives 2 & 4)
This delightful information book details how to grow your own rainbow garden.

Drake, Jane, and Love, Ann. *The Kid's Summer Handbook*. Illustrated by Heather Collins. Ticknor & Fields, 1994. (Objectives 1 & 2)
This activity guide gives children wonderful ideas to try.

Heller, Ruth. *Plants That Never Ever Bloom*. Grosset & Dunlap, 1984. (Objectives 1 & 2)
Heller's beautiful illustrations and elegant text describe a variety of nonblooming plants.

Holmes, Anita. *Flowers for You: Blooms for Every Month*. Illustrated by Virginia Wright-Frierson. Bradbury Press, 1993. (Objectives 1, 2, & 4)
Holmes provides information and care instructions for 12 indoor plants.

Lerner, Carol. *Moonseed and Mistletoe*. Morrow Junior Books, 1988. (Objective 3)
This book lists and describes poisonous plants and their locations.

———. *Plant Families*. Morrow Junior Books, 1989. (Objective 1)
Lerner shares information about a dozen of the largest and most common plant families.

———. *Plants That Make You Sniffle and Sneeze*. Morrow Junior Books, 1993. (Objective 3)
This information book describes a variety of plants that cause allergic reactions or hay fever.

Lyon, George Ella. *A B Cedar: An Alphabet of Trees*. Illustrated by Tom Parker. Orchard Books, 1989. (Objective 2)
Each letter of the alphabet is matched with the name of a tree and its leaf.

Markle, Sandra. *Science to the Rescue*. Atheneum, 1994. (Objectives 2 & 4)
This excellent book shows current problems facing the science community and how they are being solved.

Micucci, Charles. *The Life and Times of the Apple*. Orchard Books. 1992. (Objectives 1 & 4)
Micucci provides a variety of information about apples.

Wiesner, David. *June 29, 1999*. Clarion, 1992. (Objective 4)
Colorful text and fun illustrations tell of a young girl who thinks her science experiment has gone awry.

GROUP INTRODUCTORY ACTIVITY

Preparing for the Activity: Locate Lerner's *Plant Families* and have available the following materials: poster board, markers, a variety of flowers from the local area, and a transparency depicting the parts of a flower.

Focus: Before sharing this book with your class, read the introduction carefully. Give the students some background on how plant families are determined. Be certain to stress the importance of looking closely at the parts of a plant, especially the flower. Next, have the students go to the reference section of the library and research the different parts of a flowering plant. Working in groups, students can illustrate and label the different parts of a flowering plant on their poster board. Display these posters in your classroom.

Objective: To satisfy the objectives of identifying characteristics of plants and identifying different plants, bring to class a number of plants from the same family, for example, sunflowers from the Composite Family or crabgrass from the Grass Family. Then divide students into groups to label each part of the plant and decide to which family they think the plant might belong. Make sure the groups provide reasons for their answers.

Extending Activity: Have students compare their sketches about parts of the flower to a transparency prepared by the teacher depicting parts of a flower. Have students list the similarities and differences they observed.

FOLLOW-UP ACTIVITIES FOR
TEACHER AND STUDENTS TO SHARE

1. After reading Bush's *Desert Giant: The World of the Saguaro Cactus*, divide students into five groups. Each group will research the cactus in a different way. Group 1 will list and research the animals that live in or on the live cactus, such as the Gila woodpecker, the elf owl, and the Harris hawk. Group 2 will study and record information on the animals that use the blooms of the cactus, including the butterflies, bees, doves, and bats mentioned in the story. Group 3 will find information on how humans and animals use the fruit of the saguaro cactus. Group 4 will research animals and insects that live in or on the cactus after it dies. Group 5 will make a timeline of the life of the saguaro cactus. Each group should present their information on a huge cut out of the cactus. The shape and color of the cut out should coincide with the appropriate time in the life of the cactus.

2. Before reading Bush's *Tree of Life: The World of the African Baobab*, have students find a definition and location for the word "savannah." After reading the story, have students work as an entire class to assemble a giant baobab tree to display in the library or classroom. The tree can be assembled by shaping chicken wire and covering with papier-mâché. Have each student choose an animal or insect mentioned in the book to research. The students would then need to make replicas of their animals and attach them to the tree in an appropriate place. The replicas should be in proportion to the size of the model tree. Students should be given a list of specific facts to research on their animal, including how they use the tree, what they eat, and their average size and average life expectancy. Put the students' information together in a book about the baobab tree for other students to read.

3. Before beginning this activity, have available a wide variety of tree leaves. After reading Lyon's *A B Cedar: An Alphabet of Trees*, give each student a leaf. If leaves are unavailable in your area, ask students to write a friend or relative to send leaves. Explain that they will be making one page to be used in a classroom book of leaves. Provide each student with a piece of 8½" x 11" oaktag, markers, and glue. Each page of the classroom book will need to contain the following information:

- Name of the leaf
- Average height of the tree from which it comes
- Part of the country where the tree grows
- Average size of the leaf
- Care instructions for the tree
- Scientific name of the tree
- Sketch of the tree

Have students locate resources in the library to help find answers. Field guides would be helpful in answering their questions. Students should attach their leaf to the appropriate page in the book. Bind the finished product and display it in the library.

4. Divide students into nine groups and give each group a list of three plants mentioned in Heller's book. Ask students to determine what their three plants have in common. Have each group submit to the teacher its results, along with the names of the plants researched. After reading Heller's *Plants That Never Ever Bloom*, examine the findings of each research team. Discuss if any of the teams' findings paralleled Heller's observations. Then have each student choose one of the nonblooming plants for independent research. Have them find the following information:

- Location of plant
- Uses of plant
- Size of plant
- Sketch of plant

Allow time for students to share their information with classmates.

5. After reading Arnosky's *Crinkleroot's Guide to Knowing the Trees*, divide students into two groups. One group will list what they would find in a softwood forest. The other group will list what they would find in a hardwood forest. Take a field trip to a nearby wooded area or nature park. If no park or forest is available, a trip to a local nursery or greenhouse will work well. One group will locate deciduous trees; the other group will locate coniferous trees. Students should secure leaf samples of a variety of trees in each group, if possible. Using both their samples and information found in the media center, each group can create a book of its findings. Books can be shared with other classes.

6. Share the introduction of Lerner's *Moonseed and Mistletoe* with the entire class. Then divide students into the following groups: "Do Not Touch," "Berries," "Wildflowers," "Bushes and Trees," and "Holiday Plants." Each group should use this book and other library resources to develop a pamphlet that gives people the following information:

- Kinds of poisonous plants
- Where the plants are located
- Sketches of the plants
- What to do if someone comes in contact with the plant
- Any other information the students think might be important

Students should illustrate their pamphlets and display them in the media center.

7. Before reading Micucci's *The Life and Times of the Apple*, have each student bring one apple to class. Make sure each child knows which kind of apple he or she brought. Have this book available for students to look at prior to reading. Let each student label his or her apple with its proper name and one fact about it. Each day, choose a couple of chapters to read. Provide students with paper to make an apple journal. After reading each day, allow time for students to record one or two new facts they learned about apples. When the book is completed, have an apple fest. Instruct each student to prepare and bring an apple recipe for everyone to taste. Ask students to volunteer to ask their parents to help them create an apple recipe to share with the class.

8. Prior to this activity, collect the following materials for each student: two 6- to 8-ounce clear plastic cups, foil, and four bean seeds. After reading Wiesner's *June 29, 1999*, share with students an experiment that has been prepared by the instructor. Tell students that two bean seeds have been planted in each of the teacher's two cups. Do the following activity while explaining it: add water to one plant and add water with one drop of green food coloring to the other plant. Share this hypothesis with students: The plant that is watered with water and green food coloring will be greener than the control plant. Ask students to prepare their own hypothesis and experiment design for their bean seeds. Have each student share her or his plan with the instructor before implementing the plan. Limit students to common, nontoxic household items. Have students keep a daily log of their observations. Finally, have all students share their experiment results with their classmates. The instructor should report the findings of the example experiments as well.

9. This activity will require several months to complete. Share Creasy's *Blue Potatoes, Orange Tomatoes: How To Grow a Rainbow Garden*. Follow Creasy's directions to implement a colorful class vegetable and fruit garden. Students should begin by writing to seed catalog companies to obtain information about ordering seeds for these unusually colorful vegetables and fruits. After obtaining the seeds, follow Creasy's planting directions. When the students harvest their crops, use the recipes that Creasy provides to create a classroom feast.

10. Share pages 4 and 5 of Lerner's *Plants That Make You Sniffle and Sneeze* with the students. Investigate the area around the school, neighborhood, or local park to determine what plants grow in these areas. Use plant field guides to identify these plants before touching them. If the plants are not dangerous to touch, bring samples back to the classroom. Using Lerner's book, compare the samples with Lerner's drawings to determine if the area has plants that might make students sniffle and sneeze. This activity is best done in the spring or early fall.

11. After reading Appelbaum's *Giants in the Land*, lead a class discussion by asking students the following questions:

   • Has this problem been remedied?
   • What do we use trees for today?
   • How can we help?
   • How can major lumber companies help?

FOLLOW-UP ACTIVITIES FOR
INDIVIDUALS AND SMALL GROUPS

1. Read Lerner's *Plants That Make You Sniffle and Sneeze*. Using library resources, determine which plants cause allergies and hay fever in your area. Determine what time of year these plants are most dangerous. Make a chart depicting this information and share it with your class.

2. Reread Lyon's *A B Cedar: An Alphabet of Trees*. Use this book as a model to make your own alphabet book of flowers. Think of a clever name, such as *A B Carnation: An Alphabet of Flowers*. You could work by yourself or with several friends.

3. Reread Arnosky's *Crinkleroot's Guide to Knowing the Trees* and make a poster depicting a wide variety of trees in your area. Be sure to include the scientific name, a leaf, and a few specific facts for each tree.

4. To understand scientific procedures, read pages 5 through 7 of Markle's *Science to the Rescue* before beginning this activity. Do the activity on transferring pollen that Markle outlines on page 31. Share the results with classmates.

5. Read page 182 of Drake and Love's *The Kid's Summer Handbook*. Collect a variety of plants that you think would make interesting prints. Have an adult help you with the other materials. After making your prints, bring them to class to share with classmates.

6. Read pages 186 and 187 of Drake and Love's *The Kid's Summer Handbook*. Have a parent help you gather all the materials you will need for this project, and then follow the directions to make your plant press. After completing the press, use the pressed flowers to make notecards. Send your classmates notes using the cards you made.

7. Read the introduction through page 13 of Holmes' *Flowers for You: Blooms for Every Month*. Turn back to the plant chart on page 10 and use the information you've read to choose one of the plants that you would like to grow. You will need to purchase one of the plants and follow the directions for that specific plant. About once a month, bring your plant or a picture of your plant to share with classmates.

8. Read Chesworth's *Archibald Frisby* and carefully look at all the pictures. List everything in the book that is related to plants. Explain the pictures that accompany the pages that refer to plants. Share this book and your findings with the class.

■

HUMAN BODY

STUDENT OBJECTIVES

1. Identify the major systems of the human body, their function, care, and diseases.
2. Name and explain a variety of the problems created for individuals and society by the use of tobacco, alcohol, and drugs.
3. Explain how food supplies the body with energy.

RECOMMENDED READINGS

Bryan, Jenny. *Breathing: The Respiratory System.* Dillon Press, 1993. (Objectives 1 & 2)
This information book describes the parts, function, and diseases of the respiratory system.

————. *Digestion: The Digestive System.* Dillon Press, 1993. (Objectives 1 & 2)
This information book discusses the parts, function, and care of the digestive system.

————. *Movement: The Muscular and Skeletal System.* Dillon Press, 1993. (Objectives 1 & 2)
This information book describes nerves, muscles, bones, joints, tendons, and ligaments by outlining their functions.

————. *The Pulse of Life: The Circulatory System.* Dillon Press, 1993. (Objectives 1 & 2)
This information book describes the function, care, and problems of the circulatory system.

Cole, Joanna. *Cuts, Breaks, Bruises, and Burns: How Your Body Heals.* Illustrated by True Kelley. Thomas Y. Crowell, 1985. (Objective 1)
This information book clearly describes the body's healing processes.

————. *The Magic School Bus: Inside the Human Body.* Illustrated by Bruce Degen. Scholastic, 1989. (Objective 1)
The Magic School Bus takes a tour of the human body.

Markle, Sandra. *Outside and Inside You*. Bradbury Press, 1991. (Objective 1)
Markle uses outstanding photographs and text to describe body systems.

Ostrow, William, and Ostrow, Vivian. *All About Asthma*. Illustrated by Blanche Sims. Albert Whitman & Company, 1989. (Objective 1)
A child writes about asthma, its effects on his life, and how to deal with this disease.

Patent, Dorothy Hinshaw. *Nutrition: What's in the Food We Eat*. Photographs by William Munoz. Holiday House, 1992. (Objective 3)
This book provides descriptions of various foods and their importance to the human body.

Silverstein, Alvin, and Silverstein, Virginia. *The Mystery of Sleep*. Illustrated by Nelle Davis. Little, Brown and Company, 1987. (Objective 1)
This information book outlines many aspects of sleep and sleep problems.

Silverstein, Alvin; Silverstein, Virginia; and Silverstein, Robert. *Smell, The Subtle Sense*. Illustrated by Ann Neumann. Morrow Junior Books, 1992. (Objective 1)
This excellent information book explains the sense of smell.

Suzuki, David, with Barbara Hehner. *Looking at the Body*. Illustrated by Nancy Lou Reynolds. John Wiley & Sons, Inc., 1991. (Objective 1)
This information book provides an easy-to-understand narrative coupled with investigations for students to try.

Terkel, Susan Neiburg. *All About Allergies*. Illustrated by Paul Harvey. Lodestar, 1993. (Objective 1)
This excellent reference book explains the hows, whys, and whats of allergies.

Tomb, Howard. *MicroAliens: Dazzling Journeys with an Electron Microscope*. Photographs by Dennis Kunkel. Illustrations by Tracy Dockray. Farrar, Straus and Giroux, 1993. (Objective 1)
Fantastic photographs show the world through the eye of an electron microscope.

Wiesner, David. *June 29, 1999*. Clarion, 1992. (Objective 3)
A young girl launches a vegetable experiment with a surprise ending.

GROUP INTRODUCTORY ACTIVITY

Preparing for the Activity: This project will take several weeks to complete. Read both Markle's *Outside and Inside You* and Cole's *The Magic School Bus: Inside the Human Body* to the students. Have the following materials available: poster board, markers, old magazines, scissors, paste, colored pencils, crayons, sequins, beads, fabric scraps, string, cotton balls, watercolors, brushes, and any other art materials available in the classroom.

Focus: Before reading, tell students that they will become specialists in one of the parts of their bodies. Ask them to listen as you read to determine which body part they would like to investigate. After reading, ask for volunteers for each body part in the story and any others that pique student interest.

Objective: To satisfy the objectives on body systems and the problems of tobacco, alcohol and drugs, the students will research their body parts by using library resources to investigate a variety of facts and problems. Students should answer the following questions:

- What is this body part's major function, and does it have any secondary functions? If so, explain them.
- How does this body part look?
- What is it made of? Where is it located?
- How does this body part do its job in the body?
- What can harm this body part?
- What will happen to you if this body part is harmed?
- How does a person take care of this body part in order to prevent problems?

Supply students with the materials listed previously. Explain that their task is to make two posters: one showing how their body part looks and works and the other illustrating proper care of the body part. This second poster will be used in making a video entitled "A Journey Through the Human Body." Secure a video camera and videotapes for this project. Ask the library media specialist in the school to help with this project or solicit the help of a parent with a video camera. Explain to students that they will be presenting a short video documentary about their body part. Their job will be to describe to the audience, their peers, the body part, its function, and ways to keep it healthy. The students will need to use the information gathered for their poster as the narrative for their tape segment. Students' posters will be pictured to assist in explanations as the taping occurs. Students may wish to find additional pictures to be projected while they are speaking. Present the videos to the class and to other classes in your building.

Extending Activity: Hold a "Journey Through the Human Body" event as a closing activity for this project. The finished video, consisting of each student's two- to four-minute segments, could be played for parents or other classrooms. Students' posters could be displayed in the classroom. Books used as resources for this unit could also be displayed. Body-nourishing refreshments could be prepared by students.

FOLLOW-UP ACTIVITIES FOR
TEACHER AND STUDENTS TO SHARE

1. Read several portions of Cole's *Cuts, Breaks, Bruises, and Burns: How Your Body Heals* with students. For example, ask the class "What is a bruise?" and give them opportunities to answer. Then read them the chapter entitled "What Is a Bruise?" Read as many sections over the next few days as possible. Ask students to create brochures that describe or illustrate first aid procedures for any of the following: cuts and scrapes, bumps, burns, nosebleeds, broken bones and sprains, and bruises. Supply students with colored paper, fine markers, pens, colored pencils, and magazines to cut up for pictures. A computer writing and publishing program could also be used for this project. Students will need to use library resources to find safety procedures. Have students share their information with the class. Display brochures in the library or classroom.

2. Share the following sections of the Ostrows' *All About Asthma:* "Stuck with Asthma," "What Asthma Is," and "What Asthma Isn't." Find a person with asthma in your community who is willing to be interviewed by students. Before the class interview, share the Ostrows' book with the person to be interviewed and ask each student to write down two questions he or she has about asthma. Screen the questions and ask students to refine them. On the day of the interview, ask a student or several students to be the question readers. After the interview, ask students how they felt about this activity. It might also be interesting to have a doctor who cares for asthma patients come to the class to be interviewed on another day. The same procedure would work for that visit.

3. Read the first five chapters of Terkel's *All About Allergies* over several different sittings. Ask each student to interview a person with allergies. Have the students ask the following questions and any others the class might generate:

   - What are you allergic to?
   - How long have you been allergic to _____?
   - How old were you when you discovered your allergy?
   - What happened to let you know you were allergic?
   - What treatment do you use?

Have students share their interview results with the class.

4. Share several sections of the Silversteins' *The Mystery of Sleep* and ask each student to keep a sleep diary that includes the following:

- Time I went to bed:
- Time I woke up:
- Hours of sleep:
- Did I wake up in the night? How many times?
- Did I dream?
- Do I remember the dream?
- Do I feel rested? Or am I tired?
- Did I get tired at the end of the school day?

Instruct each student to keep a diary for two weeks. At the conclusion of this time, have students chart their hours of sleep each night. Ask them to form a hypothesis about the number of hours of sleep needed. Compare class results and ask students if they can draw any conclusions about the appropriate number of hours of sleep for students their age. Ask them to find documentation supporting their ideas.

5. Prior to this activity, ask students to collect oatmeal boxes and coffee tins. Share the first three chapters of the Silversteins' *Smell, The Subtle Sense* over several days. After the reading, divide students into an even number of small groups ranging from three to five members. Ask groups to select and bring six or seven items to to be used in a classroom smell experiment. Remind students about the information they have learned from the Silversteins' books about types of smells. Suggest that each group may want to include smells from several of the categories outlined in the book. After cleaning out the coffee tins and oatmeal boxes, the teacher should put each of the students' items into one of the containers. Each container's contents should be clearly labeled on the bottom. Next, divide all containers equally among the groups. Have each group work with another group. At different times, each group member from one group will be blindfolded and asked to identify all the smell containers of the other group. Each group will need to complete this in one class period, so that student discussion cannot influence the performance of individual group members. The group whose containers are being smelled will need to record the responses for each student in the other group. Then, during a different class period, the groups should trade roles. Again, the group whose containers are being smelled will need to record the responses for each student in the other group. After all smell tests are completed, have groups share with one another the true identity of the smells. Have students use their data to determine which types of smells

were most easily identifiable. Ask students if they can make any conclusions about smells from their data.

6. This project requires students to work independently on a one- to two-week project. Each student will need permanent, fine-tip markers, a camera film caddy, and about 10 to 12 frames of clear 35mm film. (Film can be purchased commercially. If clear film is unavailable, use clear slides.) After students have completed their work, a slide projector or a 35mm filmstrip projector will be necessary to view student work. Share small, interesting facts from the following four information books by Jenny Bryan: *Breathing: The Respiratory System, Digestion: The Digestive System, Movement: The Muscular and Skeletal System,* and *The Pulse of Life: The Circulatory System.* Have each student select one of these systems to investigate. Each student will need to collect facts about their body system. Have students select from the following areas to form their reports: description, function, care, diseases, and little-known facts. Provide each student with a storyboard so that she or he can plan each frame of the production. This storyboard can simply be a large piece of white paper divided equally into 10 to 12 sections. In each section, students will draw or letter the square just as it will be viewed. Thus, the first square will contain the title and producer. Remind students to keep it simple and write in the bottom of each square what their accompanying narration will be. Finally, have students present their production to the class.

7. Before reading Patent's *Nutrition: What's In the Food We Eat,* prepare a large, triangular sheet of kraft paper on a bulletin board in the classroom. Ask students to brainstorm what this triangle might be. Explain to students that this is the Food Guide Pyramid. Begin by reading one chapter a day to students. As each chapter is shared, have students jot down foods mentioned in that particular chapter. After sharing each chapter, have students write the foods in the appropriate section of the pyramid. Bring foods or packages of foods into the classroom and have students decide what nutritional value these foods might have.

8. After reading Wiesner's *June 29, 1999,* divide students into pairs and give each pair one of the vegetables mentioned in the story. Instruct students to find out what vitamins or minerals the community would be filled with if the story were true. Allow time for students to share their information with the class. Next, have students find out the proper amounts of the vitamins and minerals they should have in their diets. Share this information with the class. Have students make a class chart to show the vitamin and mineral needs of a healthy fourth or fifth grade student.

FOLLOW-UP ACTIVITIES FOR
INDIVIDUALS AND SMALL GROUPS

1. You will need a partner for these activities. Read pages 47 through 57 of Suzuki's *Looking at the Body*. Do the three activities on the heart. After you have practiced, demonstrate them for your classmates.
2. You will need a partner for these activities. Read pages 66 through 71 of Suzuki's *Looking at the Body*. Do the two activities on the digestive system and share your findings with your classmates.
3. You will need four or five classmates to help you with these activities. Read pages 75 through 86 of Suzuki's *Looking at the Body*. Do the four activities on the brain and nervous system. After you have completed the experiments, share your findings with your classmates.
4. Read pages 59 through 75 of Tomb's *MicroAliens: Dazzling Journeys with an Electron Microscope*. Be sure to also look at and read the captions that go with each photograph. Borrow a microscope from your teacher. Using the microscope, look at your finger, fingernail, and the inside and outside of your hand. Ask a classmate to do the same. Then take turns looking at each other's fingers, fingernails, and hands through the microscope. Write down or draw any differences that you see.

■

EARTH SCIENCE

STUDENT OBJECTIVES

1. Describe how the surface of the earth is constantly changing because of wind, water, volcanoes, earthquakes, ice, and heat.
2. Name and describe the three kinds of rocks that make up the earth's crust (igneous, sedimentary, metamorphic).
3. Describe the characteristics and development of the different types of rocks.
4. Classify types of clouds.

RECOMMENDED READINGS

Baylor, Byrd. *Everybody Needs a Rock*. Illustrated by Peter Parnall. Charles Scribner's Sons, 1974. (Objectives 2 & 3)
Baylor and Parnall create a beautiful book about finding a special rock.

Chesworth, Michael. *Archibald Frisby.* Farrar, Straus and Giroux, 1994. (Objectives 1, 2, 3, & 4)
The reader follows Archibald Frisby, a boy who loves science, through a variety of adventures.

Cole, Joanna. *The Magic School Bus Inside the Earth.* Illustrated by Bruce Degan. Scholastic, 1987. (Objective 1)
Ms. Frizzle and her students take a trip inside the earth to learn about rocks and soil.

Gibbons, Gail. *Caves and Caverns.* Harcourt Brace, 1993. (Objective 1)
This informational book describes caves and caverns.

Lauber, Patricia. *Volcano: The Eruption and Healing of Mount St. Helens.* Bradbury Press, 1986. (Objective 1)
Photographs, drawings, and text explain the devastation caused by Mount St. Helens.

Markle, Sandra. *Science to the Rescue.* Atheneum, 1994. (Objectives 1 & 4)
This excellent book shows current problems facing the scientific community and how these problems are being solved.

McMillan, Bruce. *The Weather Sky.* Farrar Straus and Giroux, 1991. (Objective 4)
This valuable information book depicts and explains cloud types and air patterns.

McNulty, Faith. *How to Dig a Hole to the Other Side of the World.* Illustrated by Marc Simont. HarperCollins, 1979. (Objectives 1 & 2)
McNulty cleverly takes the reader through the layers of the earth.

Parker, Steve. *Rocks and Minerals.* Dorling Kindersley, 1993. (Objectives 1, 2, & 3)
This handbook for young students describes a variety of rocks and minerals.

Simon, Seymour. *Mountains.* Morrow Junior Books, 1994. (Objectives 1, 2, & 3)
This information book describes how mountains are formed, their composition, and differences in mountain ranges and habitats.

———. *Storms.* Mulberry, 1989. (Objectives 1 & 4)
This information book describes conditions that create storms.

———. *Weather.* Morrow Junior Books, 1993. Illustrated by Ann Neumann and photographs by Seymour Simon, et al. (Objective 4)
This book describes the main types of weather and clouds.

Symes, R.F. *Rocks & Minerals*. Alfred A. Knopf, 1988. (Objectives 2 & 3)
Photographs and text give fascinating facts about rocks and minerals.

Van Rose, Susanna. *Volcano and Earthquake*. Alfred A. Knopf, 1992. Objectives 1, 2, & 3)
Photographs and text describe causes and effects of earthquakes and volcanoes.

GROUP INTRODUCTORY ACTIVITY

Preparing for the Activity: Read several selections from Van Rose's *Volcano and Earthquake*, including "An Unstable Earth," "When a Mountain Explodes," "Seafloor Spreading," and "When the Earth Moves." Have students listen for ways that the earth is constantly changing.

Focus: Tell students that this book discusses two kinds of natural disasters. Show students photographs from Lauber's *Volcano: The Eruption and Healing of Mount St. Helens*. Have available to students a variety of materials that include information on specific volcanoes and earthquakes, such as Pompeii or Mount St. Helens. Have each student select a specific volcano or earthquake to research. Provide each student with a Disaster Investigator's License. The license should be on a computer-generated form that looks similar to a passport. The student's picture should be placed on the license, which should include the following:

DISASTER INVESTIGATOR'S LICENSE

Name:

Specialty: (volcanoes or earthquakes)   PICTURE

Previous experience: (Allow students to make up their own brief histories, related to their speciality.)

Current Assignment: (Here, they would fill out the name of the disaster they are currently researching.)

License Number: (Here, they would use the date of the disaster; for example, Mt. Vesuvius erupted on August 24 in A.D. 79. Thus, the license number might be 824A.D.79.)

Next, provide each student with a disaster description form that includes the following:

Name of disaster:

Type of disaster: (earthquake or volcano)

Investigator:

Investigator's license number:

Date of disaster:

Location of disaster:

Deaths:

Survivors:

Amount of damage:

What made this disaster so infamous?

Rebuilding and/or relief efforts:

Past history of this volcano or of earthquakes in the region:

Explanation of how and why this disaster happened:

Other interesting facts:

Objective: To satisfy the objectives of understanding that the earth's surface is always changing, understanding that many kinds of rocks make up the earth's surface, and identifying the characteristics of the ocean, students will use their newly gained expertise as disaster investigators to create a short video program about their disaster. Secure a video camera and videotapes for this project. Ask the library media specialist in the school to help with this project or solicit the help of a parent with a video camera. Explain to students that they will be presenting a short news release on video about their disaster. Their job will be to describe the event and how it occurred to their audience, their peers. The students will need to use the information gathered for their disaster description forms as the narrative for their tape segment. Each student will need to make a poster to be pictured when their tape segment begins. Ask students to find other pictures of their disaster that will be projected while they are speaking. Present videos to the class and other classes in your building.

Extending Activity: Have a "Welcome Home, Disaster Investigators" event as a closing activity for this project. The finished tape could be presented to parents. Punch with dry ice might be reminiscent of a steamy volcano. A layered white cake with chocolate icing might resemble fault lines. Rock candy might be appropriate. Have students prepare refreshments at school. Allow them to use their imaginations with other recipes and decorations for the event. Be sure to display students' official licenses at this happening.

FOLLOW-UP ACTIVITIES FOR
TEACHER AND STUDENTS TO SHARE

1. Share Simon's *Storms*, focusing on the sections discussing clouds. Then share "Clouds" and "Watching the Weather Sky" from McMillan's *The Weather Sky*. Be sure to keep these books available for reference during this unit. During this earth science unit, have students record the type of clouds and the amount of cloud coverage each day. For this activity, divide students into three groups. Group 1 will record their observations each morning before 10 o'clock. Group 2 will record their observations each day at noon. Group 3 will record their observations each afternoon after 2 o'clock. Have each group prepare a chart illustrating their daily findings. Have a class discussion at the end of the unit comparing the findings of the three groups. Questions to ask might include:

   - At which time of day was there the most cloud coverage?
   - Was one type of cloud more prevalent than another?
   - Which time of day had the least cloud coverage?

2. After reading Baylor's *Everybody Needs a Rock*, take the students on a nature walk around the school neighborhood. Instruct students to look out for their special rock, one that, because of its characteristics, particularly catches their fancy. After students find one or more rocks, return to the school media center. Using library resources, have each student determine the following information about the rock he or she selected: kind of rock, type of rock (igneous, metamorphic, sedimentary), and characteristics of this kind of rock. Students can then put all of this information on poster board to display and share with their class. Their rocks could be attached to the poster board as well.

3. Share Gibbons' *Caves and Caverns*, then ask students if they have ever visited a cave or know of any caves. Make a list of where they went and what they saw. Explain to students that they are going to do in-depth research on a specific cave or cavern. Give them a list of caves or caverns to choose from. This list might include:

   - New Mexico's Carlsbad Caverns National Park
   - Alabaster Caverns in Oklahoma
   - Luray Caverns in Virginia
   - Ice Cave in New Mexico
   - Wyandotte Caves State Recreation Area in Indiana
   - Moaning Cavern in California
   - Cave of the Winds in Colorado
   - Marengo Cave in Indiana

- Blanchard Springs Caverns in Arkansas
- Onondaga Cave in Missouri
- Meramec Caverns in Missouri
- Ohio Caverns
- Bluespring Caverns in Indiana
- Penn's Cave in Pennsylvania
- Lost Sea in Tennessee
- Natural Bridge Caverns in Texas

Have students use the library to find the address of the tourism bureau of the state in which their cave is located. Then have them write letters asking for information about their cave. They will also need to use library sources for information for this project. After they have compiled their information, have students develop travel posters inviting visitors to their cave. The posters should include the name of the cave, its location, age, and description, how it was discovered, how it developed, and what it is famous for. Students will need poster board, markers, and pictures of their cave (these might be taken from brochures sent by the states' tourism bureaus).

4. Before reading McNulty's *How to Dig a Hole to the Other Side of the World*, provide students with large white paper and pencils. Tell students they will need to go to the library, find a picture of the earth's core, and sketch it on their paper. After students have completed their sketches, read McNulty's book. Tell students to listen for information about, and the names of, each layer of the earth's crust. As they listen to the story, have students label their sketches with the names of each layer and the facts about each layer that they learned from the reading. When the reading is finished, each student should stand up and share one fact about the earth's core, beginning with the earth's outer crust.

5. Prior to this activity, write the following sets of questions and instructions on 4" x 6" cards, one set to a card:

- What does "sedimentary" mean? Give several examples of sedimentary rocks and show pictures of these rocks. Bring in an example or several examples of this type of rock. Are any rocks of this type used as gemstones? If so, give an example. (Explain that gemstones are stones used in jewelry. Give some examples.) Make a chart showing or explaining how this type of rock develops.
- What does "metamorphic" mean? Give several examples of metamorphic rocks and show pictures of these rocks. Bring in an example or several examples of this type of rock. Are any

rocks of this type used as gemstones? If so, give an example. Make a chart showing or explaining how this type of rock develops.

- What does "igneous" mean? Give several examples of igneous rocks and show pictures of these rocks. Bring in an example or several examples of this type of rock. Are any rocks of this type used as gemstones? If so, give an example. Make a chart showing or explaining how this type of rock develops.

Read Cole's *The Magic School Bus Inside the Earth*, then divide students into groups of three or four, giving each group a card with one of the sets of questions and instructions on it. In some cases, more than one group will have the same set. Ask groups to use library resources to complete their tasks. Have the groups share their results with the class.

6. Share the selections "Crystals," "Gemstones," "Building Stones," and "Fossils" from Symes' *Rocks & Minerals*. Ask students to be listening for information about a rock or mineral that particularly interests them. Tell students that this book discusses many kinds of rocks and minerals. Have available to students a variety of informational materials on rocks and minerals. Have each student select a specific rock or mineral to research. Provide each student with an Amateur Geologist License. The license should be on a computer-generated form that looks similar to a passport. The student's picture should be placed on the license, which should include the following:

AMATEUR GEOLOGIST LICENSE

Name:

Specialty: (igneous, metamorphic, or sedimentary rocks)

PICTURE

Previous experience: (Allow students to make up their own brief histories related to their speciality.)

Current Assignment: (Here, they would fill out the rock or mineral they are currently researching.)

License Number: (Here, they might use the first three letters of the name of their rock or mineral followed by its hardness rating, or the element symbol and atomic number, if appropriate. Be sure the student explains the license number.)

Next, provide each student with a rock and mineral description form that includes the following:

Name of rock or mineral:

Type of rock or mineral (igneous, metamorphic, or sedimentary):

Investigator:

Investigator's license number:

Places where this rock or mineral is found:

Ways the rock or mineral is used and examples:

Unusual facts about this rock or mineral:

Unusual features of this rock or mineral:

Historical references (famous events or times or locations where this rock played an important role):

Explanation of how and why this rock or mineral was formed:

Other interesting facts:

Students will use their newly gained expertise as amateur geologists to create a short video program. Secure a video camera and videotapes for this project. Ask the library media specialist in the school to help with this project or solicit the help of a parent with a video camera. Explain to students that they will be presenting a short information blurb on video about their rock or mineral. Their job will be to share the information they have gathered with the audience, their peers. The students will need to use the information gathered for their rock or mineral description forms as the narrative for the tape segment. Each student will need to make a poster to be pictured when their tape segment begins. Ask students to find other pictures of their rock or mineral or objects actually made of the rock or mineral to be projected or displayed while they are speaking. Present the videos to the class and to other classes in your building.

7. Read the section of Simon's *Weather* that discusses clouds and cloud formations. After the reading, have students list the three basic shapes of clouds on the chalkboard. Beside each shape, have students indicate the meaning of that type of cloud. Next, have students list the cloud words that mean a rain cloud, high clouds, and a mid-level cloud. The book

gives two examples of how these names are combined to indicate clouds that have characteristics of both. Ask students to combine names to create a list of different types of clouds on the chalkboard. Ask the school librarian to videotape weather forecasts from across the nation. If a channel that displays only weather is available, it would be an excellent resource for this purpose. Each day, show students a different weather broadcast and ask students to listen for cloud names or other indications of cloud types. Discuss their findings.

8. Share Simon's *Mountains* and then ask students if they have visited any mountains. Make a list of what they saw and where they went. Explain to students that they will be doing in-depth research on a specific mountain or a mountain range, which they will select from the the following list:

McKinley	Whitney
Pikes Peak	Matterhorn
Vesuvius	Kilimanjaro
Everest	K2
Nanga Parbat	Dhaulagiri
Aconcagua	Olympus
Rainier	The Andes
The Rockies	The Appalachians
The Himalayas	

Have students use library resources to find out the following information about the mountain or mountain range they select:

Name of the mountain or range:
Location:
Age:
Height:
Width at base:
What type of matter is the mountain or range composed of?
Has it been climbed?   Details of the climb:
Is it famous? If so, why?
Unusual facts:

Ask students to use their findings to create a brochure about their mountain or range.

FOLLOW-UP ACTIVITIES FOR
INDIVIDUALS AND SMALL GROUPS

1. Reread the portion of Simon's *Weather* about clouds. Now read the remaining pages of the book. Share with classmates several new facts you learned about snow, hail, dew, or frost.

2. Reread the portion of Simon's *Weather* about clouds. Draw the various kinds of cloud formations mentioned in the book. Use a separate piece of paper for each cloud formation. Then write the name of each cloud formation on small slips of paper. Share the cloud pictures and names with other students. Let them try to match the correct name with the correct cloud formation.

3. Read the portion of Symes' *Rocks & Minerals* related to rocks used as jewelry. Select one gem that you are interested in researching. Explain the properties of that gem, including its color and hardness. Determine where it was first used as a gemstone and why. Find pictures of this gem used as jewelry.

4. Read Simon's *Storms*. Keep a weather diary for one month. Each day, indicate the average temperature, the types of clouds, the weather conditions, and the humidity, and write a brief comment indicating your opinion of each day's weather. Share your diary with classmates.

5. Reread the sections of Van Rose's *Volcano and Earthquake* that were shared in class, and then read the rest of the book. Using library sources, including magazines and newspapers, find the latest earthquake or volcano eruption that has happened closest to you. Share the details of this disaster with your classmates.

6. To understand scientific procedures, read pages 5 through 7 of Markle's *Science to the Rescue* before beginning this activity. Then read pages 40 through 43 of Markle's book; these pages discuss the dangers and the damage inflicted by hurricanes and tornadoes. Design the severe storm kit for your family that Markle describes on page 43. Share your procedure with your classmates.

7. Read Chesworth's *Archibald Frisby* and look carefully at all the pictures. List everything in the book that is related to earth science. Share this book and your findings with the class.

8. Read pages 16 through 19 of Parker's *Rocks and Minerals*. Follow the directions on page 19 to make a model of the way a mountain moves. Share your model, along with an explanation, with your class.

9. Read pages 30 and 31 of Parker's *Rocks and Minerals*. Try the activity on page 31 to see if the rock you selected is chalk. Share your findings with your class.

■

SPACE

STUDENT OBJECTIVES

1. Describe specific rocket voyages and the characteristics of space travel.
2. Study rockets and space travel.
3. Compare the effect of gravity with the effect of lack of gravity.
4. Investigate other space phenomena.

RECOMMENDED READINGS

Anderson, Joan. *Richie's Rocket*. Photographs by George Ancona. Morrow Jr., 1993. (Objectives 2 & 3)
Richie takes his spacecraft into space and discovers the phenomenon of space travel.

Baird, Anne. *Space Camp: The Great Adventure for NASA Hopefuls*. Photographs by Robert Koropp. Morrow Junior Books, 1992. (Objective 1)
This is a day-by-day account of a week at Space Camp.

Branley, Franklyn M. *Shooting Stars*. Illustrated by Holly Keller. HarperCollins, 1991. (Objective 4)
After clearly describing shooting stars, Branley provides readers with interesting facts about the sites of meteorite landings.

Drake, Jane, and Love, Ann. *The Kid's Summer Handbook*. Illustrated by Heather Collins. Ticknor & Fields, 1994. (Objective 4)
This activity guide provides wonderful ideas for children to try.

Hall, Katy, and Eisenberg, Lisa. *Spacey Riddles*. Illustrated by Simms Taback. Dial Books, 1992. (Objectives 1, 2, 3, & 4)
Hall and Eisenberg create fun riddles about the solar system, rockets, and astronauts.

Irvine, Joan. *Build It with Boxes.* Illustrated by Linda Hendry. Morrow Junior Books, 1993. (Objectives 1 & 2)
Irvine provides many fun projects to make with boxes.

Levy, Elizabeth. *Something Queer in Outer Space.* Illustrated by Mordicai Gerstein. Hyperion Books. 1993. (Objectives 2, 3, & 4)
Levy shares a clever story about the first dog in outer space.

Mayers, Florence Cassen. *The National Air and Space Museum ABC.* Harry N. Abrams, Inc., 1987. (Objectives 1, 2, & 4)
Photographs from the Smithsonian and brief descriptions provide a lot of information in this ABC book.

Polacco, Patricia. *Meteor!* G.P. Putnam's Sons, 1987. (Objective 4)
Polacco gives a colorful account of one town's reaction to a meteor.

Ressmeyer, Roger. *Astronaut to Zodiac: A Young Stargazer's Alphabet.* Crown, 1992. (Objectives 1, 2, & 4)
This alphabet book provides detailed information on space-related topics.

Ride, Sally, and O'Shaughnessy, Tom. *The Third Planet: Exploring the Earth from Space.* Crown Publishers, 1994. (Objectives 1, 2, & 4)
This information book offers many glimpses of Earth from the space shuttle.

————. *Voyager: An Adventure to the Edge of the Solar System.* Crown Publishers, 1992. (Objective 2)
This book provides the reader with detailed information from the Voyager I and II missions.

Simon, Seymour. *Look to the Night Sky: An Introduction to Star Watching.* Puffin, 1979. (Objective 4)
Simon outlines the hows and whys of star watching.

————. *Our Solar System.* Morrow Junior Books, 1992. (Objectives 1 & 2)
This information book gives an overview of our solar system and discusses specific space missions.

Stott, Carole. *Night Sky.* Dorling Kindersley, Inc., 1993. (Objective 2)
This excellent handbook explains how to look at the sky and what to look for.

GROUP INTRODUCTORY ACTIVITY

Preparing for the Activity: Locate a copy of Ressmeyer's *Astronaut to Zodiac: A Young Stargazer's Alphabet.* Prepare 26 index cards with one letter of the alphabet clearly printed in the left-hand corner of each card. Also have 26 sheets of 12" x 18" white construction paper available.

Focus: Give each student one index card and one piece of construction paper. Tell each student that they will be making a page to add to a classroom book about space. Their job is to choose a word that begins with the letter on their card. The teacher could provide students with an alphabetical list of terms related to space that includes the vocabulary in Ressmeyer's book. Or the teacher could have the students create a class list by asking the class to brainstorm the list of space terms from which students could make selections. Their word must relate to space. Instruct students to research their word and write down information about their word on their index card. Next, they will glue their index card to their white sheet of construction paper and illustrate their chosen space word.

Objective: To satisfy the objectives of identifying famous scientists and astronauts, studying rockets and space travel, and investigating other space phenomena, share pages from the students' book and pages from Ressmeyer's book beginning with the letter A. It will take several days to get through both books. When students have chosen the same word used in Ressmeyer's book, compare information to see what is the same and what is different between the two books.

Extending Activity: After reading through both books, have students choose one thing they would like to learn more about and provide the class with several facts on their chosen subject.

FOLLOW-UP ACTIVITIES FOR
TEACHER AND STUDENTS TO SHARE

1. Read Baird's *Space Camp: The Great Adventure for NASA Hopefuls* to your students over a six-day period. Explain to students that each day a different chapter of the book will be read. Tell them what the subject for the next day will be and that they should come prepared to ask questions and share one fact about that day's subject. Each chapter takes a look at different areas of space camp and technology. Be sure to give the name of the chapter so that the students can prepare. The first chapter is entitled "Astronaut Training." Instruct students to write down one question they would like to ask an astronaut and one fact they already know about astronauts. Their questions and facts will be discussed the next day. If possible, have students visit a local space camp.

2. After reading Polacco's *Meteor!*, have students find information on where meteors have crashed in the U.S. An almanac would be a good place to find this information. Then have students write letters to the chambers of commerce in those cities to find out local reactions and stories about the meteors. Compare their information with the information provided in Polacco's book. To help students with their search for meteorites, read

Branley's *Shooting Stars*, which talks about specific locations where meteorites have landed.

3. Locate Ride and O'Shaughnessy's *Voyager: An Adventure to the Edge of the Solar System* and Simon's *Our Solar System*. Have these books available for students to use during this activity. Explain to students that, during this activity, they will be interviewed as former members of a NASA mission team. Each student will need to select a mission that they are interested in studying. Students could choose from Apollo missions, Voyager missions, or space shuttle missions. Before presenting the following worksheet, share short selections from the books you located to allow students to begin thinking like crew members. Each student will then need a one-page worksheet that includes the following information:

INTERVIEW QUESTIONNAIRE FOR NASA CREW MEMBER

Which mission were you a part of?

When did this mission take place?

What was the purpose of your mission?

Who were your colleagues?

What was your job? (students may give information about the job they would most like to have)

Describe a typical day.

Give details about any unique events that happened during your mission.

Each student should find several pictures related to their mission.

After students have completed their questionnaires, group students into pairs and have the pairs practice interviewing one another. When students are ready, ask the library media specialist or a parent with a video camera to videotape the interviews. Some students will enjoy having their faces on the screen; others will prefer to talk in the background while pictures of their mission are being projected. Allow pairs to work together on the actual taping. Invite parents to view your NASA interviews by holding a "Lunar Lunch" event. Students could make refreshments for this event, including Moon Cheese Rollups (made from Swiss cheese rolled around pretzel sticks) and Mars sandwiches (made from round shapes of white bread covered with cream cheese dyed red using food coloring). Students can brainstorm other food ideas.

4. After reading Anderson's *Richie's Rocket*, explain to students that they will be building a rocket in the classroom. Have each student draw a design for the class rocket and have the class view the finished designs. Allow students to select one design to be used as the model for the class

project. Allow students to brainstorm what materials they will need for this project. Materials might include cardboard refrigerator boxes, foil, butter lids, and aluminum pie plates. Have students volunteer to secure some of the items. Give students plenty of time each day to work on building the rocket. It may be helpful to divide students into work teams. These might include teams to build the control panel, booster rockets, and fuel tanks. When this project is completed, invite other classrooms to view the class rocket.

5. Read Levy's *Something Queer in Outer Space* and have each student select an animal, other than a dog, to occupy a rocket. Ask students to prepare a newspaper article as if they were a scientist in charge of animal observation in space. Student's articles should include the effects of gravity, problems of daily living, and adaptations necessary for an animal in outer space. Make sure students include a clever title for their newspaper article. Compile students' articles into a class newspaper and make copies for each student.

6. Share Hall and Eisenberg's *Spacey Riddles* with students. Have each student write and illustrate her or his own space riddle using the same format provided by Hall and Eisenberg. Topics for riddles might include astronauts, space missions, rockets, and planet facts.

7. Read several passages from Simon's *Look to the Night Sky: An Introduction to Star Watching* to students. Focus on passages that describe the more unusual celestial occurrences, such as the aurora borealis, solar eclipses, occulations, and comets. Have each student choose one celestial phenomenon to research. Explain to students that they will prepare a pamphlet that describes and explains the phenomenon they have chosen. The pamphlet should include information on how a person might observe the occurrence, a picture or drawing of the occurrence, and any other pertinent information. Remind students that almanacs might be helpful in researching their topic. Finished pamphlets should be on display in the classroom.

8. Before sharing Mayers' *The National Air and Space Museum ABC*, write the words used for each letter of the alphabet on separate slips of paper. Let each child choose one slip of paper and find out several facts about the item on her or his slip. Then share Mayers' book. After each letter, allow students time to share their information and compare it with the information in the book.

9. Over several days, read various passages from Ride and O'Shaughnessy's *The Third Planet: Exploring the Earth from Space*. After sharing, provide students with paper and pencil and have them write the most interesting things they learned from this book. Allow 10 to 15 minutes for this activity. Next, ask students to share one item they thought was particularly

interesting. Discuss the purposes of other shuttle missions. Finally, allow students to write down their ideas for upcoming shuttle missions.

FOLLOW-UP ACTIVITIES FOR INDIVIDUALS AND SMALL GROUPS

1. Locate Stott's *Night Sky*. Read pages 56 through 59 and do the activities on page 59 to understand how a rocket blasts off. Practice this activity and then demonstrate it for your class.
2. Read page 128 in Drake and Love's *The Kid's Summer Handbook*. Follow the directions to create a reflecting telescope at home. Use your telescope to look at the moon and stars. Write down your observations and share them with your classmates.
3. Read page 129 in Drake and Love's *The Kid's Summer Handbook*. Follow the directions on how to observe meteors. Document how many meteors you see in 30 minutes. Do this for five nights and then compare and graph your results to share with your class.
4. Read pages 69 through 71 of Irvine's *Build It with Boxes*. Gather the materials and follow the directions to make the moon suit. You will need to get some help from a parent or teacher for parts of this project. Bring your suit to school and show classmates.

■

ENERGY AND MOTION

STUDENT OBJECTIVES

1. Name and describe the forms of energy, including wind, sunlight, water, fossil fuel, atomic, and wood.
2. Construct and demonstrate the use of simple machines.
3. Investigate matter.
4. Explain and demonstrate the basic principles of motion.

RECOMMENDED READINGS

Berger, Melvin. *Our Atomic World*. Illustrations by Anne Canevari Green. Photographs by Photo Resources, et al. Franklin Watts, 1989. (Objective 1) Berger provides an explanation of atoms.

Cobb, Vicki. *Gobs of Goo*. Illustrations by Brian Schatell. HarperCollins, 1983. (Objective 3)
Cobb investigates the function of gooey things.

————. *More Power to You!* Illustrated by Bill Ogden. Little Brown and Company, 1986. (Objective 1)
Cobb briefly discusses many forms of energy.

————. *Why Doesn't the Earth Fall Up? and Other Not Such Dumb Questions About Motion*. Illustrated by Ted Enik. E. P. Dutton, 1988. (Objectives 1 & 4)
This fun book asks common questions and provides answers about motion.

Irvine, Joan. *Build It with Boxes*. Illustrated by Linda Hendry. Morrow Junior Books, 1993. (Objective 2)
Irvine describes creative projects to make with boxes.

Lampton, Christopher. *Bathtubs, Slides, Roller Coaster Rails: Simple Machines That Are Really Inclined Planes*. Illustrated by Carol Nicklaus. Millbrook Press, 1991. (Objectives 2 & 4)
This information book beautifully describes and illustrates inclined planes and their properties and uses.

————. *Marbles, Roller Skates, Doorknobs: Simple Machines That Are Really Wheels*. Illustrated by Carol Nicklaus. Millbrook Press, 1991. (Objective 2)
This information book beautifully describes and illustrates wheels and their properties and uses.

————. *Sailboats, Flagpoles, Cranes: Using Pulleys as Simple Machines*. Illustrated by Carol Nicklaus. Millbrook Press, 1991. (Objective 2)
This information book beautifully describes and illustrates pulleys and their properties and uses.

————. *Seesaws, Nutcrackers, Brooms: Simple Machines That Are Really Levers*. Illustrated by Carol Nicklaus. Millbrook Press, 1991. (Objective 2)
This information book beautifully describes and illustrates levers and their properties and uses.

Lindbergh, Reeve. *If I'd Known Then What I Know Now*. Illustrations by Kimberly Bulcken Root. Viking, 1994. (Objective 2)
A father has lots of trouble fixing up around the house.

Macaulay, David. *The Way Things Work*. Houghton Mifflin, 1988. (Objectives 1 & 2)
This excellent book highlights machines, the principles on which they operate, and different principles of energy.

Markle, Sandra. *Power Up: Experiments, Puzzles, and Games Exploring Electricity*. Photo illustrations by Bob Byrd. Atheneum, 1989. (Objective 1) This information book combines a historical account of electricity with experiments and challenges for students.

————. *Science to the Rescue*. Atheneum, 1994. (Objective 2)
This excellent book highlights current problems facing the scientific community and how those problems are being solved.

Walpole, Brenda. *175 Science Experiments to Amuse and Amaze Your Friends: Experiments! Tricks! Things to Make!* Illustrated by Kuo Kang Chen and Peter Bull. Random House, 1988. (Objectives 1, 2, & 3)
This experiment book uses easy-to-follow directions and valuable illustrations to cover a wide variety of topics.

GROUP INTRODUCTORY ACTIVITY

Preparing for the Activity: Read a chapter of Cobb's *More Power to You!* over a six-day period. After each chapter is read, ask students questions. Cobb ends each chapter with a framework that allows a teacher to lead a class discussion before beginning a new chapter.

Focus: Explain to students that they will become energy specialists in the next few weeks. Have available to students a variety of materials that include information on specific types of energy, such as solar energy, nuclear energy, geothermal energy, sound energy, atomic energy, electrical energy, fossil fuel energy, light energy, chemical energy, and kinetic energy. Have each student select a specific type of energy to research. Provide each student with an Energy Specialist License. The license should be on a computer-generated form that looks similar to a passport. The student's picture should be placed on his or her license, which should include the following:

ENERGY SPECIALIST LICENSE

Name:

Specialty: (type of energy)   PICTURE

Previous experience: (Allow students to make up their own brief histories related to their speciality.)

Current Assignment: (Here, they would fill in the name of the type of energy they are currently researching.)

License Number: (Here, they would use a code for the type of energy. An example might be SOL 101 for a solar energy specialist.)

Next, provide each student with an energy description form that includes the following:

Type of energy:

Investigator:

Investigator's license number:

Dates of investigation:

Explanation of this type of energy:

Locations where this type of energy is used:

Specific uses:

How powerful is this type of energy?

How widely is it used?

Types of conservation methods:

Cost of this type of energy:

Advances made in this type of energy during this decade:

Are there experiments demonstrating this type of energy that can be easily shown in a classroom? If so, describe them in detail.

Other interesting facts about this type of energy:

Objective: To satisfy the objectives of understanding the forces of a variety of types of energy and how they were discovered, students will make a video presentation sharing the results of their investigations. Secure a video camera and videotapes for this project. Ask the library media specialist in the school to help with this project or solicit the help of a parent with a video camera. Explain to students that they will be presenting a short news release on video about a specific type of energy. Their job will be to describe the type of energy, its power and uses, and conservation measures to the audience, their peers. The students will need to use the information gathered for their energy description forms as the narrative for their tape segment. Each student will need to make a poster to be pictured when their tape segment begins. Ask students to find other pictures of their type of energy to be projected while they are speaking. Students may wish to demonstrate their type of energy on the video, if possible. Present the videos to the class and to other classes in your building.

Extending Activity: Have an energy extravaganza as a closing activity for this project. The finished tape could be presented to parents. Allow students to create foods for the event. Be sure to display students' official licenses at this event. A culminating activity for this energy extravaganza might be an energy panel. Invite public relations persons from the electric, gas, and other local power sources to participate in a question-and-answer forum. Supply panelists with student-generated questions prior to the event. Limit this part of the program to 20 or 30 minutes.

FOLLOW-UP ACTIVITIES FOR TEACHER AND STUDENTS TO SHARE

1. Prior to reading the first chapter of Cobb's *Gobs of Goo*, ask students to list gooey things. Write their responses on the chalkboard. Now read "Gooey Stuff" on pages 1 through 4 of Cobb's book. Divide the class into four groups and give each group a chapter from Cobb's book— "Greasy Goo," "Sticky Goo," "Slimy Goo," and "Warm Goo." Ask each group to assign its members the following roles: reader, recorder, materials coordinator, and investigators. Explain that the reader will be responsible for reading the assigned chapter to all group members. The recorder will be required to make a list of materials needed to perform the investigation and generate an outline of the steps of the experiment. The task of the materials coordinator will be to see that group members bring the supplies for the investigation. The investigators will be responsible for performing the actual experiment. Explain to students that these roles are only their primary responsibilities, and that they may help in any other ways necessary for the successful implementation of the experiment. Have each group perform and explain their experiment to the class. Remind groups to briefly describe how their goo is used in everyday life.

2. Locate a copy of Cobb's *Why Doesn't the Earth Fall Up? and Other Not Such Dumb Questions About Motion*. Have available the following materials: a small, easy-to-roll ball, a marble, an old bowling ball, a half-dozen eggs, a half-dozen apples, and a swing set. Divide students into six small groups and give each group an index card on which is printed one of the following six questions from Cobb's book (these questions are Cobb's chapter titles):

   - Why Does a Rolling Ball Stop Rolling?
   - Which Falls Faster, a Bowling Ball or a Marble?
   - Why Can't You Stand an Egg on Its End?
   - We Say That an Apple Falls Down to Earth. Why Doesn't the Earth Fall Up to the Apple?
   - Which Takes Longer, a Big, High Swing or a Small, Low Swing?
   - What Is a Swinging Object Good For?

Each group will need to develop a hypothesis reflecting what they believe to be the answer to the question. This hypothesis should be recorded by a group member. Each group should create an investigation that attempts to answer their question. Each group should perform experiments to determine if their hypothesis matches their experiment results. Have each group perform and explain their experiment to the class. Remind groups to briefly describe how their results relate to everyday life.

3. Introduce Lampton's *Seesaws, Nutcrackers, Brooms: Simple Machines That Are Really Levers* by asking students if they know what seesaws, nutcrackers, and brooms have in common. If students guess that these objects are all levers, ask them to name other types of levers. Now read pages 7 through 17 and demonstrate the investigations outlined. Divide the class into three groups. Using Lampton's book, let two of the groups describe and demonstrate second-class and third-class levers, respectively. Let the third group find examples of first-, second-, and third-class levers. This group should bring and demonstrate several examples of their findings.

4. Introduce Lampton's *Marbles, Roller Skates, Doorknobs: Simple Machines That Are Really Wheels* by asking students if they know what marbles, roller skates, and doorknobs have in common. If students guess that these objects are all wheels, ask them to name other types of wheels. Explain to students that there are several types of wheels: gears, ball bearings, and wheels with axles. Divide the class into three groups and assign each group one of these types of wheels to research. Allow students to begin their wheel research by using Lampton's book. Suggest that the students use library resources to find more examples of their type of wheels. Have each group describe and demonstrate gears, ball bearings, and wheels with axles. Each group should use at least one investigation from Lampton's book.

5. Introduce Lampton's *Sailboats, Flagpoles, Cranes: Using Pulleys as Simple Machines* by asking students if they know what sailboats, flagpoles, and cranes have in common. If students guess that these objects all use pulleys, ask them to name other types of machines that use pulleys. Explain to students that there are several types of pulleys: a fixed pulley, a movable pulley, and a block and tackle. Divide the class into three groups and assign each group one of these types of pulleys. Allow students to begin their pulley research by using Lampton's book. Suggest that the students use library resources to find more examples of their type of pulley. Have each group describe and demonstrate a fixed pulley, a movable pulley, and a block and tackle. Each group should use at least one investigation from Lampton's book.

6. Introduce Lampton's *Bathtubs, Slides, Roller Coaster Rails: Simple Machines That Are Really Inclined Planes* by asking students if they know what bathtubs, slides, and roller coaster rails have in common. If students guess that these objects are all inclined planes, ask them to name other inclined planes. Take several days to read and demonstrate the investigations on pages 7 through 24 of Lampton's book. Explain to students that there are two types of inclined planes: screws and wedges. Ask students to work in pairs on two tasks. First, have each pair of students determine why a screw and a wedge can be classified as inclined planes. Next, suggest that students use library resources to find examples of wedges and screws. Give students one or two class periods to finish their tasks. Bring students back together as a class and ask them to give reasons why they believe a screw and a wedge are inclined planes. Record their rationale on the chalkboard and ask them to list examples of the screw and the wedge.

7. Introduce Markle's *Power Up: Experiments, Puzzles, and Games Exploring Electricity* by reading pages 1 through 6. Demonstrate the experiment explained on page 6. Work through the book with students over a period of a few weeks. Be sure to let students try the bulb search and the circuit challenge.

8. After reading Lindbergh's *If I'd Known Then What I Know Now*, ask students to help list the areas that were troublesome for the father. The list should include roof, plumbing, electricity, cradle, kitchen, chimney, wallpaper, kitchen furniture, and barn. Ask students to choose one of these areas. Explain to students that they will need to write the area they choose at the top of a sheet of paper. Then they will need to state the problem the father was having with their particular area and outline how they would fix their particular problem. Ask students to share their finished papers with the entire class.

9. Before showing students pages 44 through 46 of Irvine's *Build It with Boxes*, have students begin collecting and bringing to class a large variety of boxes, tubes, and small balls about the size of a golf ball. After showing these pages, write the name of each of the golf activities on the board. Divide students into eight groups and let each group complete one of the golf activities. Some of these mazes are ramps, levers, and inclined planes. Supply each group with boxes, masking tape, and scissors. After each group has completed its activity, bring the activities together to make a mini golf course. Allow each group of students to work their way through the golf course.

FOLLOW-UP ACTIVITIES FOR
INDIVIDUALS AND SMALL GROUPS

1. You may want to ask for the help of several friends for this project. Read pages 116 and 117 in Walpole's *175 Science Experiments to Amuse and Amaze Your Friends: Experiments! Tricks! Things to Make!* and practice the experiments that demonstrate swinging. Show the experiments to your class.

2 You may want to ask for the help of several friends for this project. Read pages 114 and 115 in Walpole's *175 Science Experiments to Amuse and Amaze Your Friends: Experiments! Tricks! Things to Make!* Practice the experiment that demonstrates how a lever works and show it to your class.

3. You may want to ask for the help of several friends for this project. Read pages 110 and 111 in Walpole's *175 Science Experiments to Amuse and Amaze Your Friends: Experiments! Tricks! Things to Make!* Practice the experiments that demonstrate wheels and gears and show them to your class.

4. You may want to ask for the help of several friends for this project. Read pages 108–109 in Walpole's *175 Science Experiments to Amuse and Amaze Your Friends: Experiments! Tricks! Things to Make!* Practice the experiments that demonstrate how an inclined plane works and show them to your class.

5. To understand scientific procedures, read pages 5 through 7 of Markle's *Science to the Rescue* before beginning this activity. Then read pages 36 through 39, which outline the problems that have arisen from more people trying to communicate with one another. Design a communication network for you and a partner who is located at the opposite side of the building. Follow Markle's suggestions on page 39.

6. Read Berger's *Our Atomic World* to find out more about atoms and their role in our world. Share several interesting facts about atoms with a classmate.

7. Select and read a section of Macaulay's *The Way Things Work* that highlights a type of machine. Explain to your classmates how the machine you chose works. You might want to prepare a diagram or demonstration of the principle on which this machine operates.

8. Select and read a selection from Macaulay's *The Way Things Work* that explains a form of energy. Explain how this form of energy works and provide a list of common uses of this energy form.

■

ECOLOGY

STUDENT OBJECTIVES

1. Describe how a food chain works.
2. Give examples of endangered plants and animals around the world and explain why they are endangered.
3. Name and describe jobs related to the conservation of natural resources.
4. List a variety of environmental problems and describe their impact on the world.

RECOMMENDED READINGS

Ancona, George. *Riverkeeper*. Macmillan, 1990. (Objective 3)
Black-and-white photographs and text chronicle the environmental efforts of John Cronin, the riverkeeper of the Hudson River.

Anderson, Joan. *Earth Keepers*. Photographs by George Ancona. Harcourt Brace and Company, 1993. (Objectives 2, 3, & 4)
Black-and-white photos document pollution rescue missions by earth keepers.

Appelbaum, Diana. *Giants in the Land*. Illustrated by Michael McCurdy. Houghton Mifflin, 1993. (Objectives 2, 3, & 4)
This moving historical account chronicles how humans altered the life cycles of the great giant pines of the United States.

Baker, Jeannie. *Window*. Greenwillow, 1991. (Objective 4)
Beautiful collages vividly illustrate pollution problems.

Base, Graeme. *The Sign of the Seahorse*. Harry N. Abrams, Inc., 1992. (Objectives 2 & 4)
A grouper villain tries to poison the coral reef home of many fish.

The Big Book for Our Planet. Written by Aliki, et al. Illustrated by Aliki, et al. Dutton Children's Books, 1993. (Objectives 2 & 4)
This volume contains a selection of beautiful and moving short stories, illustrations, and poems that focus on our planet, Earth.

Brother Eagle, Sister Sky: A Message from Chief Seattle. Illustrated by Susan Jeffers. Dial, 1991. (Objectives 2 & 4)
Beautiful paintings illustrate the poetic and dramatic words of Chief Seattle.

Cherry, Lynne. *The Great Kapok Tree: A Tale of the Amazon Rain Forest.* Harcourt Brace Jovanovich, 1990. (Objectives 1, 2, 3, & 4)
Gorgeous illustrations help to tell the story of a young man's decision not to cut down a tree in the rain forest.

————. *A River Ran Wild.* Harcourt, Brace & Company. 1992. (Objectives 1, 2, 3, & 4)
A chronology of the Nashua River depicts its care, demise, and rebirth.

Cone, Molly. *Come Back, Salmon.* Photographs by Sidnee Wheelwright. Sierra Club Books for Children, 1992. (Objectives 2, 3, & 4)
Cone tells the true story of an elementary school that adopts a creek and saves the salmon.

Cowcher, Helen. *Rain Forest.* Farrar, Straus and Giroux, 1988. (Objectives 1, 2, 3, & 4)
Cowcher provides readers with a simple explanation of problems and their consequences in the rain forest.

Darling, Kathy. *Manatee on Location.* Photographs by Tara Darling. Lothrop, Lee & Shepard, 1991. (Objective 2)
This beautiful book describes the life and habits of the Florida manatees from the viewpoint of their human friends.

Dvorak, David, Jr. *A Sea of Grass: The Tallgrass Prairie.* Macmillan, 1994. (Objectives 2, 3, & 4)
Dvorak uses beautiful photographs to illustrate the tallgrass habitat.

The Earth Is Painted Green: A Garden of Poems About Our Planet. Edited by Barbara Brenner. Illustrated by S.D. Schindler. Scholastic Inc., 1994. (Objective 4)
This beautiful collection of poems and illustrations depicts the fragility and beauty of the Earth.

Elkington, John; Hailes, Julia; Merkower, Joel; and Hill, Douglas. *Going Green: A Kid's Handbook to Saving the Planet.* Illustrated by Tony Ross. Puffin Books, 1990. (Objectives 2, 3, & 4)
This excellent resource and project guide for older elementary students provides practical suggestions for saving the planet.

Fleisher, Paul. *Ecology A to Z.* Dillon Press, 1994. (Objectives 1, 2, 3, & 4)
This excellent reference tool provides researchers with definitions, addresses, and other sources.

Florian, Douglas. *Discovering Trees*. Charles Scribner's Sons, 1986. (Objective 2)
Florian provides details on the habitats of a variety of trees.

George, Jean Craighead. *The Missing 'Gator of Gumbo Limbo: An Ecological Mystery*. HarperCollins, 1992. (Objectives 1, 2, 3, & 4)
A young homeless girl in the Everglades becomes curious about a missing alligator.

————. *One Day in the Tropical Rain Forest*. Illustrated by Gary Allen. Thomas Y. Crowell, 1990. (Objectives 2, 3, & 4)
This story tells of a young rain forest Indian and a scientist's quest for a nameless butterfly.

————. *Who Really Killed Cock Robin?: An Ecological Mystery*. HarperCollins, 1991. (Objectives 1, 2, 3, & 4)
A young boy is called upon by the Mayor to find out what is really behind the mysterious death of Cock Robin.

Gerstenfeld, Sheldon L., V.M.D. *The Aquarium Take-Along Book*. Illustrated by Paul Harvey. Viking, 1994. (Objectives 2, 3, & 4)
This excellent information book not only takes the reader on an aquarium tour, but develops the reader's awareness of the environmental problems facing the world's water habitats.

Gibbons, Gail. *Nature's Green Umbrella: Tropical Rain Forest*. Morrow Junior Books, 1994. (Objectives 1, 2, 3, & 4)
Gibbons identifies and describes rain forests and explains the dangers that threaten them.

Handelsman, Judith F. *Gardens from Garbage: How to Grow Indoor Plants from Recycled Kitchen Scraps*. Illustrated by Anne Canevari Green. Millbrook Press, 1993. (Objectives 1 & 4)
This activity book carefully outlines how to start an indoor garden from food scraps.

Hirschi, Ron. *Where Are My Prairie Dogs and Black-Footed Ferrets?* Photographs by Erwin and Peggy Bauer and others. Bantam Books, 1992. (Objectives 2, 3, & 4)
Hirschi uses photographs and text to describe the plight of grasslands and prairies.

Irvine, Joan. *Build It with Boxes*. Illustrated by Linda Hendry. Morrow Junior Books, 1993. (Objectives 2 & 4)
Irvine provides many fun projects to make with boxes.

Kennedy, Teresa. *Bringing Back the Animals*. Illustrated by Sue Williams. Amethyst Books, 1991. (Objective 2)
Brief glimpses are provided into the lives of a variety of endangered animals from around the globe.

Lowery, Linda. *Earth Day*. Illustrations by Mary Bergherr. Carolrhoda, 1991. (Objectives 2, 3, & 4)
Lowery's poetic story details former Senator Gaylord Nelson's Earth Day.

Markle, Sandra. *Science to the Rescue*. Atheneum, 1994. (Objective 4)
This excellent book shows current problems facing the scientific community and how these problems are being solved.

McVey, Vicki. *The Sierra Club Kid's Guide to Planet Care and Repair*. Illustrated by Martha Weston. Sierra Club Books for Children, 1993. (Objectives 2 & 4)
This guide describes environmental problems and ways to help solve them.

Pandell, Karen. *Land of Dark, Land of Light: The Arctic National Wildlife Refuge*. Photographs by Fred Bruemmer. Dutton's Childrens' Books, 1993. (Objectives 1, 2, & 4)
Beautiful photographs and text describe the fragility of arctic wildlife.

Patent, Dorothy Hinshaw. *Yellowstone Fires: Flames and Rebirth*. Photos by William Munoz and others. Holiday House, 1990. (Objectives 1, 2, & 4)
Patent explains the importance of the 1988 Yellowstone fires to the forest ecology.

Pratt, Kristin Joy. *A Walk in the Rainforest*. Dawn Publications, 1992. (Objectives 2 & 4)
An alphabet book takes a tour of the rain forest.

Stwertka, Eve, and Stwertka, Albert. *Cleaning Up: How Trash Becomes Treasure*. Illustrations by Mena Dolobowsky. Julian Messner, 1993. (Objectives 3 & 4)
This information book discusses the basics of recycling.

Willow, Diane. *At Home in the Rain Forest*. Illustrations by Laura Jacques. Charlesbridge Publishing, 1991. (Objective 2)
Willow provides brief yet informative text about life in the Amazon Rain Forest.

Wu, Norbert. *Beneath the Waves: Exploring the Hidden World of the Kelp Forest*. Chronicle Books. 1992. (Objectives 2, 3, & 4)
Wu chronicles the fragility, importance, and care of the kelp forest habitat.

Yolen, Jane. *Welcome to the Greenhouse.* Illustrated by Laura Regan. G.P. Putnam's Sons, 1993. (Objectives 2, 3, & 4)
Beautiful text and lush illustrations depict life in the rain forest.

GROUP INTRODUCTORY ACTIVITY

Preparing for the Activity: Begin this unit of study by reading Cherry's *A River Ran Wild* to students. Discuss who and what was involved in this river clean-up operation. Now read one chapter of Cone's *Come Back, Salmon* each day for six days.

Focus: Ask questions after each day's reading. These questions might include:

- Do we have areas like Pigeon Creek near our school?
- Can we clean up our environment (the school) or another neighboring environment in any significant way?
- How do you feel about the work these students did? Do you think that their work was important, and why?

After the books are read, use brainstorming techniques to come up with an environmental project in the school area. Two examples of such a project might be a "Clean the School Campaign" or an "Eco-Awareness Week." Students should be prompted to list ways to help in the campaign for the week. Some ideas might be:

- Friday playground pick-up
- Paper recycling bins in each classroom and teacher work area
- Aluminum can recycling bags
- Cafeteria recycling program
- Environmental awareness posters
- Student-designed environmental awareness buttons
- Slide show showing the school as it looked both before and after the "Clean the School Campaign"

Objective: To satisfy the objectives of developing an awareness of endangered plants and animals around the world and developing a heightened awareness of environmental problems and their impact on the world, allow students to implement one of their project ideas. Students would need to come to a consensus on which idea to implement if there were more than one.

Extending Activity: Invite a local environmentalist to visit the school. The local chamber of commerce, city offices, or a local university might be helpful in locating an appropriate speaker. Ask students to list questions or issues they would like discussed by an environmentalist. Submit these questions to the speaker prior to his or her appearance date. Culminate this activity by reading Anderson's *Earth Keepers*. Discuss how these people made a difference. Allow interested students to write to one of the environmental organizations listed on the last page of the book to find out more information on how they can help.

FOLLOW-UP ACTIVITIES FOR
TEACHER AND STUDENTS TO SHARE

1. Prior to sharing Baker's *Window*, cut construction paper window frames in the shape of the classroom or school windows. These need to be as large as the windows in the classroom. Make a "window frame" for every two students in the classroom. Share Baker's *Window* and explain to students that they will be making collages depicting the view out the classroom window. Their collages will show this scene riddled with pollution. Remind students to consider all types of pollution. The teacher will need to have a variety of materials available for the collage.

2. Before reading Cherry's *The Great Kapok Tree: A Tale of the Amazon Rain Forest*, share Cowcher's *Rain Forest*. Explain to students that this is a simplified tale of problems in the rain forest. After the reading, ask students two questions: What is the problem? and How did the animals react? Now share Cherry's book and tell students that they will be listening for all the animals mentioned in the story and that they will need to make a list. After the reading, be sure to share the end papers and the information about the author on the book jacket. Ask students what message the author is trying to convey. Have students build a Kapok tree. The tree can be made out of chicken wire shaped into a tree and covered with papier-mâché, or out of huge cardboard cut outs and covered with kraft paper. Have students include each of the animals mentioned in the book. Students should also do presentations explaining how each animal would be affected if the tree was gone. Do the presentations for other classes. Include the following animals in the tree: sloth, anteater, tree porcupine, jaguar, tree frog, toucan, macaw, cock-of-the-rock, monkey, bee, and boa constrictor.

3. Share *Brother Eagle, Sister Sky: A Message from Chief Seattle* with students. Generate a class discussion that includes why students think that Chief Seattle's words were not understood long ago, but are now. Ask students to work in small groups. Have each group select a type of pollution—land, air, water, or noise. Have each group use magazines to find pictures depicting their type of pollution. Using slide film and a 35mm camera, have groups take slides of the magazine pictures to create a group

slide presentation. To provide accompanying narration, students should complete the following statement on paper:

To prevent {air, land, water, noise} pollution, people can or should

_____.

Each group should have a number of responses equal to the number of students in the group. Each group should select a narrator who will read all group members' responses into a tape recorder. This tape can be played as slides are presented. Invite other classrooms to the slide presentations.

4. Share Lowery's *Earth Day* with students. Ask each student to find, re-search, and discuss one current piece of state, city, or federal environ-mental legislation. This discussion should include who or what will be affected by this legislation and how. Sources for research might include magazines, newspapers, and online services. Have an Earth Day Celebra-tion at your school.

5. Take several days to share Base's *The Sign of the Seahorse* with students. After the reading, ask students to select their favorite scene for the class to act out. Assign parts in the scene selected. Extra students may act as the deep sea creature of their choice. Allow students time and materials to create costumes and backdrops for the play. After several dress re-hearsals, present the play to other fourth and fifth grade students.

6. Before reading Willow's *At Home in the Rain Forest*, divide the class into four groups. Assign each group one of the following titles: Plants, In-sects, Mammals, and Reptiles. Instruct the students to record the names of members of their assigned groups mentioned in the story. After read-ing the story, have each student research one item on their list. After researching, students should share a picture and interesting facts about their insect, plant, mammal, or reptile with the class.

7. Before reading Kennedy's *Bringing Back the Animals*, provide each stu-dent with a piece of paper that includes the following headings: Animal, Location, Cause of Extinction, Importance, and What's Being Done. Explain to students that Kennedy provides information on 12 different animals. Tell students they will need to write down the specific informa-tion for each animal as the book is read. After sharing the information on the Giant Panda, fill out each column with the class. As the rest of the book is read, allow time after each animal for students to complete their charts. When the book is finished, share the addresses in the back of the book with students. Divide students into small groups and assign each group an agency to write to for more information on endangered species.

8. Begin by sharing the first part of Florian's *Discovering Trees* (read up to the part about habitat). Tell students to listen for information about how a tree grows and other specifics. Then provide students with maps and names of trees. Instruct students to find information about specific trees. Students should be able to find information on where the tree grows and why that is the best place for the tree to grow. Have students work in small groups to find information on the following trees: baobab, bald cypress, gingko, date palm, sugar pine, and pin oak. Then read the ending of Florian's book to see if their information is correct. Provide the class with a map of the world. Have each group make a simple cut out of their tree and place it on the map where their tree was originally located.

9. This activity will take several weeks to complete. Locate Dvorak's *A Sea of Grass: The Tallgrass Prairie*, Hirschi's *Where Are My Prairie Dogs and Black-Footed Ferrets?*, Pandell's *Land of Dark, Land of Light: The Arctic National Wildlife Refuge*, Patent's *Yellowstone Fires: Flames and Rebirth*, Wu's *Beneath the Waves: Exploring the Hidden World of the Kelp Forest*, and Yolen's *Welcome to the Greenhouse*. Share each of these books with students. The entire book can be read, or only specific chapters. Have students listen for information about a variety of habitats. After all the books have been shared, instruct each student to select a specific habitat to research. The students will need to have access to a wide variety of library resources, including magazines, newspapers, books, and online sources. Provide each student with a Habitat Investigator's License. The license should be on a computer-generated form that looks similar to a passport. The student's picture should be placed on the license. This license should include the following:

HABITAT INVESTIGATOR'S LICENSE

Name:

Specialty: (type of habitat—rain forest, grasslands, etc.)

Previous experience: (Allow students to make up their own brief histories related to their speciality.)

PICTURE

Current Assignment: (Here, they would fill out the name of the habitat they are currently researching.)

License Number: (Here, they would use a number and letter combination of their own choice. An example might be ECO120.)

Next, provide each student with a habitat description form that includes the following:

Name of specific habitat: (i.e., Amazon Rain Forest)

Type of habitat: (grasslands, rain forest, etc.)

Investigator:

Investigator's license number:

Location of habitat:

Plants that inhabit this habitat:

Animals that inhabit this habitat:

Types of threats that endanger this habitat:

Types of endangered species:

Extent of damage to habitat at this time:

Environmental rebuilding and/or relief efforts:

Organizations that can be contacted regarding environmental rebuilding:

Other interesting facts about the habitat:

Students will use their newly gained expertise as habitat investigators to create a short video program about their habitats. Secure a video camera and videotapes for this project. Ask the library media specialist in the school to help with this project or solicit the help of a parent with a video camera. Explain to students that they will be presenting a short news release on video about their habitat. Their job will be to describe the habitat, how it became endangered, and how to get involved in relief or rebuilding efforts to the audience, their peers. The students will need to use the information gathered for their habitat description forms as the narrative for their tape segment. Each student will need to make a poster to be pictured when their tape segment begins. Ask students to find other pictures of their habitat that will be projected while they are speaking. Present the videos to the class and to other classes in your building.

Have a habitat awareness event as a closing activity for this project. The finished tape could be presented to parents. Tropical punch with dry ice might be reminiscent of a steamy rain forest. A jar filled with cheese straws might resemble grasses from the grasslands. Have students prepare refreshments at school. Allow them to use their imaginations with other recipes and decorations for the event. Be sure to display students' official licenses at this event.

10. Share several selections from *The Earth Is Painted Green: A Garden of Poems About Our Planet.* Try to select a wide variety of topics to share. Include poetry about pollution, the beauty of the Earth, and plants. Ask students to write a poem about one thing about the earth that they cherish or an editorial poem encouraging people to save the planet. Invite students to share their work with their classmates.

11. Share Ancona's *Riverkeeper* with students. After sharing, have students compile a list of people in the community who are responsible for protecting a lake, river, park, or other nature area. After the list is compiled, contact one or several people on the list to come to the class and describe their job. Before the visit, have students prepare questions they would like to ask. Have students record the answers and write an article in the school newspaper using the guests' comments.

12. Locate and share Gibbons' *Nature's Green Umbrella: Tropical Rain Forest* with students. Then divide the class into three groups and have each group research a different type of rain forest. The three types mentioned in Gibbons' book are tropical rain forests, mangrove forests, and temperate rain forests. The students' research will include animals, plants, and problems common to that type of rain forest. Also, have each group make a map depicting the location of their particular rain forest type.

13. If possible, arrange a trip to a local aquarium or fish store. Read several sections of Gerstenfeld's *The Aquarium Take-Along Book* to students. Be sure to include the sections on the jellyfish and shark. Also read pages 92 through 100 to students, which highlight the importance of conserving our water and natural resources, including wetlands, coral reefs, groundwater, and specific water animals. The author gives a one-sentence description of a variety of careers in the field of marine science. The names of conservation and education organizations related to marine science are also given. Allow students to select one of the following two projects to investigate for this unit.

Project 1. Select one of the following careers in marine science to investigate:

- Aquarists
- Aquatic veterinarians
- Marine biologists
- Oceanographers
- Oceanographic engineers
- Underwater filmmakers
- Veterinary technicians

Use library resources to find the following information about the selected marine career:

- Where would you live if you chose this career?
- What training would you need?
- Describe a typical day on the job:
- If possible, interview someone who is involved in the marine sciences.

Project 2. Write to one of the organizations listed on pages 101 and 102 of this book. Ask for literature from the organization. Use library resources to find out when the organization was founded and how many members it has. Find out if this group has carried out any major environmental projects.

14. Before sharing Pratt's *A Walk in the Rainforest*, provide each student with a 4" x 6" index card with an alphabet letter and the accompanying word from the book printed on the card. Tell students to go the library and find pictures and two facts about the word on their card. When students return to the classroom, have them briefly share their information. Then read Pratt's book. Compare students' drawings and facts with those in the book. Then provide each student with an 8" x 8" square of white cloth and fabric pens or permanent magic markers. Instruct students to draw a picture representative of their alphabet letter on their cloth. Remind them to include the alphabet letter on the square. Solicit the help of a parent to sew the squares of cloth together to make a rain forest quilt. Display the quilt in a prominent place in the school.

15. Read Appelbaum's *Giants in the Land* to students. After the reading, lead a class discussion by asking students the following questions:

- Has this problem been remedied?
- What do we use trees for today?
- How can we help?
- How can major lumber companies help?

Ask students to contact a paper mill or lumber mill and inquire if the plants have any plan in place for replanting trees. The address of paper mills or lumber mills can be found in telephone books in the public library. Ask students to interview a forestry specialist, having them list questions for the interview beforehand. Interviews can be done in person, by modem, or by letter.

16. Read Sleator's "Traffic" in *The Big Book for Our Planet* and then lead a class discussion by asking students the following questions:

- What do you think Sandy did when he became a car person?
- What city do think might be the setting for this story?
- What can you do about car exhaust pollution?

17. Read Cherry's "From Island to Island" in *The Big Book for Our Planet* and then lead a class discussion by asking students the following questions:

    • What is the author trying to say to the reader?
    • What was the grandmother's purpose in telling this story?
    • Is overpopulation a problem in our world? If so, where?
    • What are possible solutions to overcrowding?

18. Using the list of environmental organizations in Elkington's *Going Green: A Kid's Handbook to Saving the Planet*, give each student an index card with the name and address of an environmental agency or organization. Ask students to write to their agency seeking information. Students gather information regarding the organization's history, purpose, membership requirements, and projects. After the information has been received, explain to students that they will each be creating an illustrated brochure that highlights the history, purpose, membership requirements, and projects of the organization. Have students share their finished brochures with the class. Ask the class to select the organization that appeared to be doing the most to aid the environment.

19. Prior to reading the landfill selection from the Stwertkas' *Cleaning Up: How Trash Becomes Treasure*, assemble the ingredients to make a model landfill for the classroom. Then share pages 19 through 26 with the class. These pages explain how a landfill works. Have students help make the model landfill described on page 24. Put the landfill somewhere in or near the classroom so that is accessible to students. Allow students to view the decomposition process. Have a blank notebook close to the model. Each day, ask two students to record their observations. It will take at least eight weeks for students to understand the process.

20. Show students pages 34 through 37 in Irvine's *Build It with Boxes*. Explain to students that they will be working on a similar project, the difference being that their rain forests will be made in refrigerator boxes. Tell students that the teacher will provide the light source to set behind their box. Next, divide the class into groups with six to eight students in each group. Have the groups meet and decide who will bring the box and what other materials they will need. Also have each group start working on a sketch illustrating what they want their finished project to look like. Allow several weeks for students to complete their projects. Display the projects in the school library.

21. Share George's *Who Really Killed Cock Robin?: An Ecological Mystery* and *The Missing 'Gator of Gumbo Limbo: An Ecological Mystery* with students. These chapter books will take several weeks to share. Each of these books discusses many different ecological issues, scientific procedures, causes

of environmental problems, and ways to solve these environmental problems. Begin with one book and share a chapter a day with students. Before beginning, provide each student with a notebook that will become her or his journal. This journal will be used for notetaking and researching. For example, before sharing *Who Really Killed Cock Robin?: An Ecological Mystery* explain to students that they will be listening to a story about the unusual death of a bird. They will need to try and help the protagonist in the story figure out the cause of the bird's death. The day before sharing the first chapter of this book, write the following words on the board: aniline dyes, DDT, carbon dioxide, carbon monoxide, insect predators, hydrocarbon, pyrethrum, rotenone, serin, and nontoxic insecticides. Explain to students that they will need to find out what each of these words or groups of words means. Tell them to jot down notes in their journals to bring to class the next day. The next day, share the first chapter of George's book. After sharing, take time to discuss the words students researched the day before. Then ask the students to respond to the following questions in their journals:

- What kinds of information did Tony keep in his notebook?
- Why was each piece of this information so important?
- What were some problems the town of Saddleboro was experiencing?

Also instruct students to write down any other information they think might be necessary in helping to find the reason the cock robin died. Do similar activities for each chapter of the book. Do the same type of activities for George's *The Missing 'Gator of Gumbo Limbo: An Ecological Mystery*. Be sure to share with students the forewords from both of these books.

22. Locate a copy of George's *One Day in the Tropical Rain Forest* for each student in the class. Explain to students that each of them will be reading and discussing this book about the rain forest. Each day, assign a specific number of pages for each student to be ready to discuss the next day. Have available a map so that students will be able to see the location of the rain forest mentioned in the book. Mark this location on the map. Provide students with journals to keep a daily reading record. Instruct them each day to include animals, problems, plants, and solutions to the problems mentioned in the story. Provide time for class discussion each day. After reading the entire book, have each student choose a project they would like to do relating to the book. Projects might include:

- a newspaper article explaining the problems of the rain forest
- a poster depicting the birds, insects, or mammals mentioned in the story
- a report done on other books about the rain forest
- another idea they have discussed with the teacher

Allow students time to share their finished projects with the class.

FOLLOW-UP ACTIVITIES FOR INDIVIDUALS AND SMALL GROUPS

1. Read the section on supporting companies that use good ecological practices on page 92 of Elkington's *Going Green: A Kid's Handbook to Saving the Planet*. Write to the Environmental Data Clearinghouse to ask for a list of the 50 best companies. Determine if any of these companies make products you use. Make a display of products made by these companies. Share your display with your class.

2. Read pages 44 through 53 of McVey's *The Sierra Club Kid's Guide to Planet Care and Repair* to learn more about acid rain. Follow the directions to create your own acid rain experiment. Explain your procedures and results to your classmates.

3. Read pages 44 through 53 of McVey's *The Sierra Club Kid's Guide to Planet Care and Repair* to learn more about endangered species. Write a letter to the president, your senator, and a representative to encourage them to support laws that protect and save wildlife.

4. Read Darling's *Manatee on Location*. Find out if there are any endangered animals in your area or state. Research where they live and why they are endangered. Write to a local or state park agency to find out what is being done to help local endangered animals. Share your findings with classmates.

5. To understand scientific procedures, read pages 5 through 7 of Markle's *Science to the Rescue* before beginning this activity. Now read pages 8 through 11. These pages discuss the problem of overpopulation of coastal cities. Draw the diagram that Markle challenges you to create. Share the problem and your diagram with your classmates.

6. To understand scientific procedures, read pages 5 through 7 of Markle's *Science to the Rescue* before beginning this activity. Now read pages 32 through 35. These pages outline the problems of pollution caused by the exhaust of transportation vehicles. Using the information on pages 34 and 35, create a nonpolluting model car and share it with classmates.

7. Read pages 7 through 11 of Handelsman's *Gardens from Garbage: How to Grow Indoor Plants from Recycled Kitchen Scraps* to understand the whys

and hows of indoor gardening from kitchen scraps. Look through the remainder of Handelsman's book. Select the kitchen scraps that you wish to grow and follow the procedures outlined in the book. After your plant is flourishing, bring the plant to school and share it with other students.

A HELPFUL RESOURCE

Fleisher's *Ecology A to Z* provides students with a great dictionary, includes lists of addresses for environmental organizations, and also includes an extensive bibliography for students and adults on books concerned with environmental matters.

NONPRINT SOURCES FOR GRADES 4-5

Prior to using any of these nonprint sources, read all of the accompanying documentation and preview the application. The literature accompanying many of these products suggests appropriate uses. Determine if the material is to be used by the entire class, by small groups of students, or by an individual student. After choosing the audience for the nonprint material selected, it will be necessary to teach students how to use the application.

LIFE SCIENCE—ANIMALS

The Great Ocean Rescue. Tom Snyder Productions. Laserdisc with optional Mac or Windows software.
This simulation allows students to learn about marine biology and oceanography.

Mammals: A Multimedia Encyclopedia. National Geographic Society, 1993. CD-ROM Mac or MS-DOS versions.
This CD-ROM program includes a wide variety of photos, movie clips, text, and maps describing the behavior of mammals.

Oceans Below. Software Toolworks. CD-ROM Mac or MS-DOS versions.
Students can explore the ocean through the eyes of a scuba diver.

Odell Down Under. MECC. Mac or Windows versions.
Students explore animals, plants, and the food chain of the Great Barrier Reef.

The San Diego Zoo Presents...The Animals! The Software Toolworks, 1992-1993. CD-ROM Mac or Windows versions.
This CD-ROM program takes the viewer through a tour of the San Diego Zoo, including highlights of over 200 animals.

LIFE SCIENCE—PLANTS

Desert Giant: The World of the Saguaro Cactus. Reading Rainbow Series, GPN, 1989. VHS videocassette.
Students view the various habitats that the Saguaro cactus provides.

Lunar Greenhouse. MECC, 1989. Apple II software.
This simulation requires students to find the optimum conditions for plant growth.

Odell Down Under. MECC. Mac or Windows versions.
Students explore animals, plants, and the food chain of the Great Barrier Reef.

HUMAN BODY

Cavity Busters. MECC, 1991. Apple II software.
This simulation allows students to investigate variables that affect healthy teeth.

InnerBody Works Jr. Tom Snyder Productions. Mac, Apple II GS, or MS-DOS versions.
This software program provides students with an interactive introduction into the human body and its systems.

Nutrition Nabber. MECC. Apple II software.
This simulation requires students to identify nutritious foods.

The Ultimate Body. Dorling Kindersley's DK Multimedia, 1994. CD-ROM Windows or Mac.
Body organs and body systems are explored through interactive questions and answers.

What Are We Eating? National Geographic Society, 1991. National Geographic Kids Network, Mac or MS-DOS versions.
This telecommunications unit fosters research and computer skills while teaching students the importance of nutrients in the foods they eat.

EARTH SCIENCE

The Great Ocean Rescue. Tom Snyder Productions. Laserdisc with optional Mac or Windows software.
This simulation allows students to learn about plate tectonics, sea floor characteristics, and geological history.

Hill of Fire. Reading Rainbow Series, GPN, 1987. VHS videocassette.
Students learn about several significant volcanic eruptions throughout history in this video.

The Magic School Bus Inside the Earth. Reading Rainbow Series, GPN, 1990. VHS videocassette.
Students explore the mysteries of caves.

Weather in Action. National Geographic Society, 1990. National Geographic Kids Network, Mac or MS-DOS versions.
This telecommunications unit allows students to investigate local and worldwide weather events through research.

SPACE

Expert Astronomer. Expert Software, Inc. Mac or MS-DOS software.
This interactive program allows viewers to search the solar system from any place and zoom to a favorite solar spot.

The Great Solar System Rescue. Tom Snyder Productions, 1992. Laserdisc with optional Mac or Windows software.
This simulation allows students to learn about the solar system.

Rocket Factory. MECC. Apple II and MS-DOS software.
This simulation game permits students to build and launch a rocket while investigating force, motion, and space travel.

Space Shuttle. Software Toolworks, 1993. CD-ROM Mac or MS-DOS versions.
Students can explore space travel through the eyes of a shuttle crew member.

Where in Space Is Carmen Sandiego? Broderbund. Mac or MS-DOS software.
Students search for Carmen Sandiego in space.

ENERGY AND MOTION

Electrifying Adventures. MECC. Apple II and MS-DOS software.
This simulation game permits students to explore electricity.

Miner's Cave. MECC, 1988. Apple II and MS-DOS software.
This simulation game permits students to explore the uses of simple machines and force.

Mystery Matter. MECC, 1988. Apple II and MS-DOS software.
This simulation game permits students to explore matter and energy, including electricity, water, and magnetism.

Pizza to Go. MECC. Apple II software.
This simulation game permits students to explore the uses of simple machines and force.

Rocket Factory. MECC. Apple II and MS-DOS software.
This simulation game permits students to build and launch a rocket while investigating force, motion, and space travel.

Simple Machines: An Introduction to the Physical Sciences for Children Ages 8–14. Science for Kids. CD-ROM for Mac and Windows versions.
This CD-ROM program allows students to explore the importance of the six simple machines throughout history.

Solar Energy. National Geographic Society, 1992. National Geographic Kids Network, Mac or MS-DOS versions.
Students are encouraged to use research skills to examine solar energy concepts throughout this telecommunications unit.

The Way Things Work. Dorling Kindersley's DK Multimedia, 1994. CD-ROM Windows or Mac.
This CD-ROM program is based on Macaulay's book of the same name. Students can tour an inventor's workshop.

ECOLOGY

Acid Rain. National Geographic Society, 1989. National Geographic Kids Network, Mac or MS-DOS versions.
Students explore the environmental issues surrounding acid rain through this telecommunications unit.

Cleanwater Detectives. MECC. Apple II software.
This simulation allows students to investigate water pollution.

Decisions, Decisions: The Environment. Tom Snyder Productions. Apple II, Mac, MS-DOS software.
This simulation game requires students to decide the fate of a town's polluted pond.

The Great Ocean Rescue. Tom Snyder Productions. Laserdisc with optional Mac or Windows software.
This simulation allows students to learn about ocean pollution.

GTV: Planetary Manager. National Geographic Society. Videodisc available for Mac, Apple IIGS, or MS-DOS.
This interactive program allows students to explore environmental issues and answers.

Too Much Trash? National Geographic Society, 1991. National Geographic Kids Network, Mac or MS-DOS versions.
Students are encouraged to use research skills to examine the problems of trash and waste disposal in our world through the use of telecommunications.

What's in Our Water? National Geographic Society, 1991. National Geographic Kids Network, MAC or MS-DOS versions.
Students explore the environmental issues surrounding water pollution in this telecommunications unit.

INDEX

Compiled by James Minkin

Index 183